One Woman's
Journey

One Woman's Journey

a portrait of
pauline vanier
foreword by jean vanier

Deborah Cowley & George Cowley

NOVALIS

Cover design: Christiane Lemire

Cover photo: L'Arche International

Layout and design: Christiane Lemire, Francine Petitclerc

Revised edition ©1993 Novalis, Saint Paul University, Ottawa

Reprinted 1994

Business Office: Novalis, 49 Front Street East, 2nd Floor,
    Toronto, Ontario M5E 1B3.

Editorial Office: Novalis, 223 Main Street, Ottawa, Ontario K1S 1C4.

Printed in Canada

Canadian Cataloguing in Publication Data

Cowley, Deborah, 1937-

    One woman's journey: a portrait of Pauline Vanier

Rev. ed.
ISBN 2-89088-639-5 (bound). — ISBN 2-89088-715-4 (pbk).

    1. Vanier, Pauline, 1898-1991. 2. Governors
general — Canada — Spouses — Biography. 3. Arche
(Association) 4. Vanier, Georges P. (Georges
Philias), 1888-1967. I. Cowley, George, 1930-
II. Title.

FC621.V36C69   1993   971.064'2'092   C93-090555-5
F1034.3.V36C69 1993

NOVALIS

Contents

Foreword

As this book reveals, my mother, Pauline Vanier, had a long, full and varied life. Towards the end of that rich life, at an age when most people seek a quiet retirement, she made an important choice. She decided to come and live with my l'Arche community in Trosly, France. She was responding to what she felt was a call from Jesus to deepen her spiritual life and to live more simply in accordance with the Gospel.

The death of my father a few years earlier had been an enormous loss for her. She and my father had lived a deeply united married life for 46 years; she thus became very lonely. My community, however, was happy to welcome her and she was truly happy with us. It was as if the community provided the ground for her fulfilment, a place where, for her final 20 years, she was able to bring together her many gifts and spiritual aspirations. In l'Arche she found a new and deeper meaning to her life.

Because I had left home at the age of 13, it was in Trosly where I lived with her for the longest period and where I got to know her best. It was a joy for me to witness her immense capacity to welcome others. She gave much love to many assistants and to visitors at l'Arche. To those with learning difficulties, she became the mother or grandmother they had lost or had never known. And she was wonderfully loved in return.

There was such a thirst in her to be loved and to love. As she grew older, this thirst became ever more child-like, and one sensed that as the frustrations of old age became greater, her longing for love became more urgent.

Like everyone else, she suffered in and from community life. There is no perfect community, and the community in Trosly is no exception to that rule! My mother was not perfect either. Sometimes she was angry with the community and with me. These clashes came also from her failing health and strength, a decline she found difficult to accept.

During her final years, however, she knew moments of great spiritual comfort. "I cannot understand," she would say, "why it is so easy to pray. The Good Lord is there, so present to me; He is so good." At other moments, she would groan and complain: "Why doesn't the Good Lord come and fetch me? Has He forgotten me?" She lived times of terrible anguish and spiritual desolation; her outbursts of anger left her feeling wretched and lonely, depressed and guilty. She seemed to live many of the contradictions a child lives, but at the same time, when a visitor arrived, she would be welcoming, interested and extremely thoughtful.

The temptation and danger would be to put my mother on a pedestal. In many ways she was placed on a pedestal by the Canadian people, and that made life more difficult for her – she had to live up to so many expectations. This book shows how deeply and beautifully human she really was. Like all of us, she had her ups and downs. She had her own personality, gifts and psychological wounds. She frequently had to make great efforts to be faithful to God and to her mission but she was clearly loved by God and was an instrument of God's love in our broken world.

Many years ago, Debbie and George Cowley asked my mother to record some of her recollections. She did this with them in 1971, when she was 73 years old. Her memory was obviously selective, recalling certain realities and forgetting others. This book is made up essentially of these tapes, put together and edited by Debbie and George, a work of care and of love. They were with my parents at Rideau Hall and a deep friendship grew between them. My mother thus placed great trust in them and shared her thoughts and memories quite simply and intimately.

While this is not a biography, I nonetheless feel it will help people identify more closely with my mother and enable them to know a little more about her life, which was so full of hope and love.

Jean Vanier
L'Arche
Trosly-Breuil, France

Preface

In 1971, when Pauline Vanier was contemplating leaving Canada for France, we persuaded her to draw on her remarkable memory and let us tape several hours of her reminiscences on what was already then a long and eventful life. An excellent biography of her late husband, Governor General Georges Vanier, had been written by Robert Speaight, but for understandable reasons it could accord little space to Pauline Vanier's distinctive experiences and impressions. Never wanting to upstage her husband, she had consistently shied away from interviews about her own story. We thought it would be a major tragedy if that life went unrecorded, especially with her own perceptive insights and lively commentary.

We taped more than 18 hours of her recollections. Always the soul of tact and discretion, she attached only one condition: that her words not be made public until the major players mentioned had passed from the scene.

As it turned out, Pauline Vanier outlived them all. We reminded her of this in the fall of 1990, and, happily, she agreed to let us transcribe the tapes with an eye towards possible publication. We made plans to travel to her home in France the following spring to seek her help in updating and expanding the transcripts. Her sudden death in March 1991 thus struck us as a double tragedy.

Jean Vanier urged us to proceed nonetheless with the compilation of this book. To cover the period since our recording, he arranged for us to talk to members of his community at l'Arche whose lives had been so deeply touched by his mother's presence. To them, to the other Vanier children who gave us invaluable help, and to many of her friends in Canada who spoke with us, we are profoundly grateful.

Thanks to them, and to our own conversations with Pauline Vanier over almost 30 years, we have a collection of her most colourful reminiscences, largely in her own words, of a bountiful 93 years.

It has been a privilege to compile these passages. It has been an even greater privilege to know and to love Pauline Vanier and to celebrate her remarkable life with this small book.

Deborah Cowley
George Cowley
Ottawa, Canada

1
Pauline Vanier: Mother to Us All

It was a cold, drizzly day in March 1991 when a tiny village in northern France bid sad farewell to a loving and much-loved friend.

Days before, on March 23, Pauline Vanier had died peacefully in her sleep, just short of her 93rd birthday.

As word of her passing spread to her native Canada, hundreds who had known her personally and thousands who had admired her from afar shared a deep sense of loss.

Her life had been as rich and full as anyone could hope for, and she lived it with an energy and intensity that amazed those who knew her. She was one of the great women of her time and for many, her death marked the end of an era when such greatness was judged by compassion and self-giving.

It was in 1972 that the widow of Georges Vanier, one of Canada's most admired governors general, renounced a quiet and comfortable life of retirement in Canada and flew to France. The fact that she was already 73 didn't stop her from embarking on a new and untried path radically different from any she had known before: to join a community called l'Arche (the Ark), in a small village northeast of Paris.

The community had been founded by her son Jean Vanier, and has become the flagship of a worldwide network of similiar communities offering a secure and caring haven for men and women with mental handicaps. Pauline Vanier hoped that at l'Arche she would find not only a home, but also a vocation for the final years of her life.

How fully she succeeded was never more evident than on that frigid March afternoon when the community's 400 members gathered in a large hall off the town's main square for a funeral service and farewell to a friend they affectionately called *Mamie* (the French term for "Granny"). Most came on foot, while the more seriously handicapped were wheeled into the hall or carried by young assistants. The last members were still arriving as two guitarists and a solitary flutist began playing Pachelbel's poignant *Canon in D*. Then a dozen white-clad priests — many of them close personal friends — gathered behind a simple altar laden with pink and white roses.

At the priests' request, Jean Vanier first addressed the gathering. "What a gift it was that she came to live here with us," he began. "Today we celebrate the joys of her life, not only at l'Arche but of all those 93 years — such beautiful, beautiful years." Priests, assistants, and the handicapped themselves joined in a procession of tributes. At the end of the service, her coffin was placed in a waiting van and, as it pulled slowly away, a chorus of voices cried, "Bye, bye, Mamie. Au revoir."

The next week, a Canadian Forces plane carried her body back to her beloved Canada. Over 300 friends and senior government officials — including Governor General Ray Hnatyshyn and former Governor General Roland Michener — filled the Notre-Dame Cathedral in Quebec City to pay their last respects.

"She was a lady of importance, yet more deeply, like all of us, she was a little child thirsting to love and be loved," her son Jean recounted at that service. He added, in words of a significance few could have realized, "She can rejoice: she has discovered she is loved herself and can herself give love for eternity." Members of the Royal 22nd Regiment, which her husband helped to found in 1914 and later commanded as colonel, escorted her coffin to the Citadel where her body was laid in a tiny chapel beside that of her husband.

No one who has ever met Pauline Vanier will forget the experience. Her tall upright figure, dazzling smile, and handsome, patrician face capped by a head of snowy-white upswept hair had become familiar to millions of Canadians. She was recognized nationally as the devoted wife of Georges Vanier, distinguished soldier, skilled diplomat and one of the most respected and loved Governors General in Canada's history.

Yet, in her own right, she was a truly exceptional person. She was blessed with a most youthful and irrepressible spirit, and the thousands of people she met from every walk of life were seldom left unmoved.

They responded to her with an outpouring of affection. She was, for example, voted Canadian Woman of the Year in a 1965 Canadian Press poll and won the prestigious Cardinal Newman Award, an honour conferred annually to Catholic laypersons for exceptional service to humanity.

In addition, she was named a Companion of the Order of Canada, the nation's highest award. Seven universities granted her honorary degrees, while countless communities across the nation named schools and colleges, parks and community centres after her. When an island in an Arctic archipelago was named *Ile Vanier* after the late Governor General, the Geographic Board promptly decided to call the island next to it *Ile Pauline*.

She was equally honoured outside Canada. For her services during World War II, for example, she received the French Legion of Honour, the Order of Malta and was also made a Dame of the Order of St. John of Jerusalem. But the international tribute that touched her most was an apricot pink rose sent to her in 1960 by the government of France. The rose was the first of a new hybrid named in her honour to recognize her postwar welfare work among the French people. Clearly delighted, she planted it in the rose garden of Government House, the Ottawa residence of the Governor General, where its descendants thrive to this day.

But it was Canadian Prime Minister Lester B. Pearson who best reflected the nationwide admiration for Pauline Vanier. In August 1967, in a most unusual honour for a non-political figure, he appointed her a member of the Queen's Privy Council — the first female non-politician ever named (entitling her thereafter to be addressed as "The Honourable"). As Pearson commented: "She was one-half of a perfect partnership in the service of Canada."

That perfect partnership was one that spanned 46 years, produced five remarkable children and carried the couple throughout times of war and peace to many world capitals — London, Geneva, Algiers, and finally Paris to head up the Canadian Embassy. There Pauline Vanier donned a second-hand Red Cross uniform and worked tirelessly to help victims of war in Europe. During their nine super-charged years, they became two of the most popular diplomatic envoys in the country and their departure was considered, by one journalist, as "almost equivalent to the removal of a Paris landmark."

When they returned to Ottawa to serve as the representatives of the country's Head of State, the vice-regal couple worked tirelessly to know and to inspire their fellow Canadians. During their nearly eight years in office, they welcomed thousands of people from every corner of the nation to Rideau Hall. They journeyed across the land — by helicopter, plane, boat, train, even by river scow on the Mackenzie River —

visiting each province regularly, as well as the Far North.

Of the thousands of people she met, Pauline Vanier most loved the children, missing no occasion to sweep them up in her arms and engulf them in a motherly embrace. Hers was a special touch that clearly delighted the young: on a visit to a Winnipeg hospital, she noticed a small boy who was shamefully embarrassed by his shortened leg. "I wish they'd shorten both of mine," she told the beaming lad, "then I wouldn't be so tall!" And during their term at the embassy in Paris, Pauline once turned up late for an important luncheon. The reason, she apologized, was simple. When she emerged from a store, she found a group of youngsters swarming around her embassy limousine. "What else could I do but bundle them all inside and take them for a ride," she explained. "We were having so much fun I completely forgot about the time!"

It was during the latter days of the Governor General's term, when doctors advised him to reduce his hectic pace, that Pauline Vanier showed her true mettle. She began working overtime to help meet the many demands of the office, and her trepidation of speaking in public never stopped her from substituting for her husband on countless occasions. Though plagued by a lifelong fear of flying, on one occasion she flew by small aircraft to Yellowknife, North West Territories, to open a medium-security prison. As was often the case, she stepped on the podium, tossed aside her prepared text and spoke spontaneously. "I had a text all ready to read you," she declared, "but I think I shall talk without it — with less head, probably, but with more heart." She did just that, and won a standing ovation from both officials and prisoners in her audience.

The special Vanier partnership was also marked by a deeply-felt concern for the welfare of the family. Sharing the view that the decline in family solidarity was the source of many of society's ills, they convened the first-ever Canadian Conference on the Family in

June 1964. The opening ceremony was held on the grounds of Government House and may well have been unique in Canadian history: on the Vaniers' initiative, it was led by a benediction pronounced in unison by leaders of 17 different religious communities. The conference resulted in the creation of the Vanier Institute of the Family, a research agency set up to strengthen the unity and integrity of the family. Its work continues today.

After George Vanier's untimely death in 1967, Pauline Vanier continued to shoulder every responsibility she could — as the first female Chancellor of the University of Ottawa, as a driving force behind the Vanier Institute and as an active patron of several social welfare institutions.

She also continued to be passionately dedicated to the concept of a united Canada. Like her husband, she was perfectly bilingual in both French and English, and together they demonstrated, especially during Quebec's separatist stirrings in the 1960s, that harmony between Canada's two founding cultures could be mutually enriching.

Even after she moved to France, she kept in close touch with her homeland. She telephoned friends in Canada almost weekly for an update on Canadian news, just as she would grill Canadian visitors to l'Arche on everything from politics and social movements to the arts and religion. She returned often to Canada; her last trip was in her 91st year and included visits to Toronto and Quebec City.

But it was at l'Arche, where she became resident grandmother, trusted confidante and devoted friend to so many, that her sense of service to others found its most complete fulfilment. "She brought the stability of her experience, age and mothering heart to a community of people often over-extended in their emotional and physical commitment to the handicapped," noted Canadian journalist John Fraser, who visited her often. "There, day in and day out, she opened her door — and her arms (the all-engulfing Vanier hug is something to behold) — to anyone in need of comfort or counsel."

This keen interest in people of all ages stretched well beyond the borders of l'Arche. When Charles Pottie, a Jesuit priest from Halifax, was preparing for his ordination, he wrote to Pauline Vanier — although they had scarcely met — and invited her to the ordination ceremony. His simple statement expressed the sentiment of many: "I feel as if in some way you are mother to us all."

Such were some of the marks of greatness that allowed Pauline Vanier to win the admiration and affection of millions of Canadians. Few know, however, that her journey was beset with self-doubt as well as faith, heartbreaks as well as joys, tragedy as well as good fortune and defeats as well as triumphs. These were all part of the long road Pauline Vanier had first to travel to reach this greatness.

Charles Archer, Thérèse de Salaberry Archer and daughter Pauline, c. 1900.

(Notman & Son, Montreal. National Archives of Canada, PA 127232.)

2
Growing Up in Edwardian Montreal (1898-1919)

Pauline Vanier's life and origins, like Georges Vanier's, were rooted in both Canada's founding nations, French and English.

She was born in Montreal on 28 March, 1898, the only child of Judge Charles Archer of the Quebec Superior Court and his French wife, Thérèse. Judge Archer was a grandson of an English gentleman-farmer from Brixham in Devon, England, and his wife a descendant of the seigneurial family of de Salaberry who first emigrated to Canada in 1730.

Pauline's mother was a surprisingly small woman given her daughter's six-foot stature, and Pauline remembered her with much affection. "She was a wonderful lady with a great sense of humour," she recalled, "but she was also a bit of a snob. She loved blue blood and she made ours out to be almost a little too blue. We had to humanize it with a little red. I guess we compromised on purple!"

Both her parents, however, had blood from other races prominent in Canada. "On father's side, the blood is much more mixed. Grandfather Archer was half Scottish and half English and his wife was half German and half French. Imagine mixing German and French wine! On my mother's side, the de Salaberry's were both French and Basque. So all in all, we were quite a mixture."

Her father was a huge man of 6'2". "He was a brilliant lawyer, but he wore himself out with work. His partner wasn't happy that he was so important in the firm and had him appointed a judge. That was when he was only 42 which was far too young. He took the job terribly seriously and was always hyperconscientious — he'd never go to the club and always kept aloof.

"People tell me he was a very able jurist and that many of his judgments are still cited in court today. But he had a difficult time. He was seen by English Canadians as being French because he had been brought up speaking French in Quebec, while French Canadians didn't consider him one of theirs — they said the name Archer marks him as English. In some ways, he was never fully accepted by either side.

"It would be hard to find two more different backgrounds and temperaments than my two parents. Father was an outdoor man who liked golf while mother was tiny and frail and had to spend a lot of time in nursing homes and hospitals. She was also more intellectual — she had a real brain — and deeply spiritual — my, she had a tremendous faith. But even with such fragile health, she lived to be 93!

"Nonetheless, they were very happy together — as happy as such different people could be."

In his later years, Judge Archer was offered the position of Lieutenant Governor of Quebec. "The job tempted him a little but, alas, he felt he could not accept. Mother's health was simply not strong enough to take on such a position. Neither, it transpired, was his: the poor man died in 1934 at only 63."

The young Pauline grew up in a big sandstone house on Montreal's Sherbrooke Street. "One of my earliest memories is of my bedroom — all pink and white with rosebuds on the curtains, an ivory-lacquered desk and a beautiful doll's house, full of miniature furniture. Since I was an only child with very adoring parents, I suspect I was spoiled rotten. At Christmas, we decorated a big tree and gave a party for needy children. Then we travelled to Quebec City to join all our cousins who gathered at grandfather's house."

Life for young people in Montreal in the early days of the century — particularly those from middle- or upper middle-class families — was governed by straight-laced Victorian morality. Children were lovingly but strictly raised. Most, like Pauline, were educated at home by governesses or at single-sex, church-run schools. Meetings between the sexes were seldom allowed before late adolescence, and even then the encounters were often formal, stilted and closely chaperoned. Pauline's experience was no exception.

"Until I was 17, I was never allowed to leave the house alone," she recalls. "I had a *femme de chambre* who followed me everywhere. She even accompanied me to my singing lessons! Luckily, they didn't continue for long: I had a strong voice but a tone-deaf ear!"

It was a lonely life for an only child and she longed to get out of her own house and visit other friends' homes. "My favourite was a friend who had a large house and a skating rink and a toboggan slide. I loved to spend the days with her. But I never wanted to invite anybody back to my house. I always felt that we couldn't give them the fun that other people gave me."

Pauline was deeply religious, even as a young girl. "I seriously thought then I would like to be a nun and was quite attracted to the idea of a religious life. When I was twelve, I heard one of our great missionaries speak about his life in the North, and I decided at once that I would join his order and live in the Arctic."

She spent four years from age eight to twelve at the Sacred Heart Convent in Montreal; the rest of her

schooling was supervised at home by private governesses who "never taught me anything and certainly
never awakened my curiosity." Even her mother took
steps to protect her from what she saw as some of the
evils of literature. "There were many books I was not
allowed to read — mother pinned the forbidden pages
together and put me on my honour not to read them.
But I did get hold of a copy of André Gide. That was
very daring in those days. But I didn't understand a
word!"

At age 15, however, her intellectual horizons wid-
ened. Pauline met a young French woman, a professor
at McGill University, who immediately developed a
keen interest in the eager young teenager. "Germaine
Grétrin was very beautiful. She had Titian hair and
brown eyes and white skin, and she was brilliant. She
took me under her wing and was to have the most
enormous influence on me."

Germaine Grétrin taught French and English literature, and both subjects were a revelation to the young
Pauline. Together they visited libraries searching for
books, then discussed them for hours. "Our language
at home was mostly French and my governess rarely
touched on literature. So I knew little about French
literature and nothing of English. It was Mlle Grétrin
who really started me off. She opened the door to a
whole new world for me."

At about the same time, Pauline's mother exposed
her to life outside her own privileged family circle to
learn how the poor lived. "She took me down to
Griffintown to visit a woman named Mrs. Daly who
looked 50 but was only in her 20s. She was a French
Canadian who at 13 had married an Irishman who
drank like a fish and stayed with her only long enough
to father a daughter, Mary-Ann. The woman suffered
from recurrent rheumatic fever, so my mother took me
down every week to do her shopping and play with
little Mary-Ann. It was a revelation to me to see how
such people lived.

"The contrast was brought home to me when, soon after, I received my first invitation to a formal ball. It was to be held at Government House in Ottawa and it was all too exciting for a young 17-year-old. My most vivid memory was of the Comptroller, Sir Richard Neville, leading me out from dinner and saying, 'Miss Archer, you know you must dance with His Excellency.' Well, I was petrified. But off I went and waltzed with the Duke of Devonshire who was then Governor General. He'd had quite a lot of port and couldn't dance very well and at the end of the dance, he said 'Miss Archer, do come and sit on the throne.' So he sat on one side and put me on the other and when I looked over at him, I discovered he'd fallen asleep! I was stuck there for almost half an hour before an aide finally came up and took me away."

Back in Montreal, Pauline was longing to exert a little independence so, at 19, she secretly signed up for a course in first aid and home nursing.

"I never told my parents I had enrolled. I even secretly ordered my uniform. Then the day before I was to report for classes, I told my mother what I had done. Her reaction was very bad: she said she was distressed that I had hidden my plans from her but I think the real reason was that she thought I was too young to work outside the home. But Father was secretly proud. When World War I broke out, he had no son who could join up and was himself too old to be accepted. So I think he was rather pleased. He arranged for me to stay with an aunt who lived close to the course and, the next morning, I took my uniform from the cupboard and presented myself for duty."

Her training was little more than the most basic course in home nursing. It thus came as a shock to be assigned as an apprentice nurse on night duty alone in a convalescent home for male army officers.

"Imagine the contrast between my protected upbringing and THIS! Much of the time, I was alone on night duty with all these men, many of whom would come in tight, and a sergeant who had no authority whatsoever. It wasn't easy and there were many frightening moments. When my father learned about the situation, he went right to the Chief Medical Officer and had me transferred. It was too humiliating."

She was moved to another section, just as the Spanish flu epidemic reached Canada in the fall of 1919 killing hundreds. "Amazingly, I never caught flu, even though I was right in the midst of it and took very few precautions. Just an aspirin whenever I got a headache. We lost a lot of our staff so we had to work double duty. In fact, we were so busy, I didn't have time to worry.

"The most heart-rending were the patients who one day would complain simply of a bad headache and you came in the next morning and found their beds empty. They had died in the night. And nearly always, it was the youngest and strongest who were struck. That was tough. Today, we have antibiotics; then, there was nothing we could use to fight back. The whole thing was quite devastating for a girl who had never seen death."

She continued her social welfare work well into her twenties, visiting families and the children of sick and wounded soldiers. But at the same time, the attractive young 20-year-old was also becoming interested in men.

"At first, I was very, very shy and would play up to them in the most stupid way. I tried to be coy but didn't know how! I was a big girl and I would try to put on airs and make myself look pale and interesting with powder and red lips, the Theda Bara sort of woman. It was so unlike me. At age 20 I was going through what girls of 14 go through now."

Little did she guess the changes that would soon transform her life. Her family was planning to leave for Europe in September 1919. That same month she was also to meet a distinguished war hero named Georges Vanier.

3
Courtship and Marriage to Georges Vanier (1919-1923)

Early in 1919, francophone society in Montreal was lionizing a brilliant young French Canadian army officer, "Tommy" Tremblay, who at 33 was already well on his way to becoming one of Canada's youngest generals. Pauline Archer had met him previously, but felt that among so many competitors for the debonair bachelor's attention, she could hardly have made much of an impression.

"Imagine my astonishment when, out of the blue, he asked me to be his partner at one of the biggest social events of the season — a party to welcome home to Canada the members of Quebec's own Royal 22nd Battalion, the famous and much-decorated 'Van Doos' regiment.

"It was all terribly exciting. Tommy was not all that good-looking, but he was certainly a charmer. I was determined to get him to tell me all about himself and his wartime experiences. But every time I asked him a question he would talk instead about one of his officers named Georges Vanier, and how this courageous soldier had lost a leg on the battlefield and had won many top medals including the Distinguished Service Order and a Military Cross for his bravery. I must confess I

Pauline Archer at 22, a year before her marriage.

was a little annoyed with this Georges Vanier for having unknowingly cramped my style with Tommy Tremblay."

Months later, she was having tea in the Ritz Hotel. "Tommy suddenly appeared at my table and said excitedly, 'Georges Vanier is here! But he's temporarily on crutches. Would you be willing to come to our table and meet him?' Fortunately the mention of crutches reminded me of who he was, and I agreed to follow Tommy." As they approached his table, Georges Vanier stood up. "He was a tall, distinguished-looking man of 31, with greying hair and moustache and such courtly manners. He gave a deep bow and said, 'Bonjour.' I remember thinking he was exceedingly handsome and sympathique, had such a charming sense of humour and a delightful twinkle in his eye. We seemed to get along quite well and he invited me to lunch the following day. Suddenly I began to realize that my interest was already beginning to shift from Tommy to Georges!"

Whether or not Pauline Archer's parents approved of this sudden new interest, she could not tell. One thing was certain, however: they reminded her that they still planned to leave a few days later for an extended vacation in France, and they were counting on her to go with them.

Pauline was crushed. Worse still was the fact that, after she told Georges of her family's insistence, he accepted the news with complete aplomb. However, he did mention casually about "giving her a small present before she left," boosting her expectations enormously.

When the gift finally arrived, it was not quite what she had envisioned. There, carefully rolled up, was a set of Georges' wartime army staff maps, every detail carefully annotated by hand so that she could visit all the battlefields he'd fought on and even retrace his footsteps.

"Some of my friends made fun of such an unromantic present, but he'd taken such obvious trouble to write

Georges and Pauline Vanier in Montreal, 1922.

in all the movements of each battle. I was thrilled and quite touched."

The Archers' ship was due to sail from Quebec City. Georges could not get leave to see them off but Pauline hoped he would send a message to await her on board. Nothing arrived. Much later she learned that in fact he had sent her flowers, but to the wrong ship! In the meantime, she was heartbroken.

"So I'm just a passing fancy to him," she said to herself. "Well, I'll show him!" And show him she did. Barely three months after her arrival in France, Pauline became engaged to a handsome French army officer who was also a distant cousin. By coincidence, he had lost an arm in the war. "Georges used to tease me about this coincidence, saying I would fall in love with anyone, as long as he was missing a limb!"

It seemed at first to be a story-book engagement: the dashing French war hero, a glittering reception with dozens of family and friends, and even, belatedly, a telegram of congratulations from Georges Vanier which cryptically read: "You will understand some day why I have not congratulated you before now."

But the thrill of the moment soon palled. "I realized almost at once that I could never really love this man, let alone be happy married to him, and that I had only accepted his proposal to spite Georges. I became more and more unhappy during the months that followed. I would cry myself to sleep every night. I'd go to Mass each morning and beg the Lord to do something, *anything*, to get me off the hook."

In spite of her apprehension, she found it impossible to contemplate breaking off the engagement. "I felt that once a promise had been made there was no way it could be broken. I didn't dare ask my mother's advice for fear she would confirm my duty to marry. I tried to convince myself that even if I couldn't love my husband, perhaps I could find fulfilment in having dozens of children. Oh my, how I suffered!

"When I think how ignorant young women of our upbringing were in those days! Most girls of my generation knew nothing at all about love, and even less about sex. Most of us had only the vaguest idea how children were born: I thought merely a kiss could be enough to cause pregnancy!"

It was four months before Pauline was able to summon the courage to break off her engagement. "My fiancé made a terrible scene, then stalked out into the night, and for days no one could find him. Everyone was convinced he must have committed suicide! Luckily he had not."

During these months in Paris, Pauline had the good fortune to be introduced by a friend to a circle of young Catholic writers — La Vie des Jeunes — who met every Tuesday for lectures and discussions.

"It was so exciting to be involved with such a fascinating group of people — in fact most of the top writers of the day, including François Mauriac. How they put up with me, I'll never know, because I wasn't anywhere near their level so I usually just kept quiet. But it was my first real taste of French literature and it was thrilling."

At the end of the summer of 1920, Pauline and her parents sailed back to Canada. Emotionally exhausted, Pauline left Montreal with relatives to recuperate in the peaceful and isolated Gaspé region of Quebec on the lower St. Lawrence. She continued to cling to the hope of renewing relations with Georges Vanier "but I couldn't think how to pick up the thread." By coincidence she happened to meet a lawyer, Walter Shanks, who worked in the same law firm as Georges and who was also vacationing in the Gaspé.

"'Miss Archer,' he said, 'I think you know Georges Vanier. He speaks of you often. Why don't we send him a postcard together?' I couldn't believe it. It was providence. That's why I believe in providence."

Pauline insisted that Walter write the message, and she added only her name at the end. "I'm still haunted by a conviction that if I had let my timidity get the better of me and not signed that postcard, I might never have seen Georges Vanier again."

Georges soon replied with the news that he was leaving his law firm in Montreal and would be rejoining the army in Quebec City. Since it would be hard to obtain leave in the first months of his new duties, would Pauline consider visiting him in Quebec?

She rushed back to Montreal to ask her parents' consent to visit Quebec City. They agreed, and arranged for relatives to act as chaperones. The couple was soon seen almost weekly dining out.

"Georges talked a lot about his childhood and the strong influence of his grandfather Maloney, a taciturn Irishman who was a difficult man of few words. I also quickly discovered how much he liked books and enjoyed nothing more than to browse through second-hand bookstores. How he loved to talk about all his favourite authors — Shakespeare and the English novelist William Thackeray. He also loved poetry; he was an extraordinary romantic and adored the works of the English poets, Byron, Keats and Shelley. Years later, I found a little red leather-covered book of Shelley's poems that he had carried in his breast pocket throughout the whole war."

By January, the couple was also taking evening sleigh rides together. This was a time when Georges would discuss with Pauline his current readings in philosophy: Henri Bergson, who contended that the world was a great conflict between the forces of life and materialism, and Ernest Psichari, who claimed that military discipline could serve as a model for Christian discipline. Pauline agreed but believed that love was more important than discipline. "I think I held my own to his satisfaction," Pauline later commented. However, she also had other things on her mind during those long sleigh rides.

"I was beginning to wonder whether or not Georges Vanier would ever pop the question. Finally, during a visit in mid-January, I told him I'd have to cut short my stay and return to Montreal the next day. It worked! He proposed to me that night. Then the next morning, he phoned and asked me somewhat hesitantly, 'Did I *really* propose to you last night?' When I assured him he had, he said simply, 'Good. I thought I'd better confirm that you had the same impression!'"

The first token he offered her, even before a ring, was a little bottle in which he had kept a clump of earth from the boot of his leg that had been amputated. "He obviously considered this a precious and symbolic possession: he was giving me something very dear to him. I found that gift not only sentimental and touching, but very romantic. I've still got that little bottle with its silver top upstairs in my bedroom."

Both agreed that it would be wise to have a long engagement. On the rare occasions when they could not be together on weekends, Georges sent her a generous bouquet of roses. For good measure, he sent one to her mother as well. Pauline's mother was completely won over, but she thought it wise to caution Georges on the characteristics of the young woman he was proposing to marry: "The intense ardour of her nature... My God, what exuberance of life, heart and soul; how impressionable — almost too much for her nervous system!"

Pauline and Georges were married on 29 September 1921. They chose Notre-Dame Basilica in Montreal for their wedding. Their friends and well-wishers filled the large church, and the couple left through an arch of swords held by Georges' fellow officers.

After the reception, they drove to the White Mountains of New Hampshire for a short honeymoon. Georges was still not comfortable driving a car with his artificial leg so his younger brother Anthony volunteered to accompany them as chauffeur. "It was a generous gesture. But by the time we'd reached our destination, Anthony was feeling so protective he refused to leave us. Georges found endless excuses to send him off on errands or would give him $5.00 to go to a movie. But back he would bounce like a bad penny. He had decided he would be very obsequious and treat us like very important people: he would bow to us, rush forward to open doors for us, pull out our chairs, until finally Georges cried out in exasperation, 'Anthony, have you gone completely mad? For goodness' sake, stop all this nonsense!'

"We laughed and laughed. Eventually Anthony joined in too — but only when we were about to return to Montreal."

From honeymoon luxury, the newlyweds soon found themselves isolated and alone in a new and strange town — Kingston, Ontario — where Georges had been sent to attend a course in the Canadian army staff college.

"Having to get by on a peacetime army officer's salary and pay for our own room and board was quite a comedown. All we could afford as lodgings was a decrepit, fifth-rate boarding house on King Street which always seemed dirty, no matter how much we cleaned it.

"We lived on a diet of bread and sausages, and our income only allowed us to buy two sausages at a time. We had a small bedroom and shared a living room, divided by a curtain down the middle, with another couple. They were a talkative pair, and with the bedroom too small for Georges to study in, you can imagine the problems he had trying to master complex military strategies in our tiny living room with nonstop conversation going on a few feet away!"

A reversal of fortune was on its way, however. Viscount Byng of Vimy had been appointed the new Governor General of Canada. Byng was a British aristocrat and an officer in the British cavalry at the outbreak of World War I. In 1916 he was put in command of the Canadian Corps serving in France and the next year he led it in a heroic victory at Vimy Ridge in northern France. He was, therefore, a popular choice among Canadians as the new Governor General.

One of Byng's first initiatives was to invite Georges Vanier to serve on his staff as an aide-de-camp, an honour usually reserved for young British officers, and never before bestowed on a French Canadian. Byng had heard much of this gallant Quebecker, and was particularly impressed by Georges' determination to continue in the army despite the loss of a leg.

Pauline, a bride of less than a month, awaited her first meeting with Lord Byng with trepidation, assuming that Lord Byng would be an august and formal personage. On their first encounter, however, the Governor General threw open his arms and embraced her in a very Canadian bear hug.

"Not only that," Pauline recalls, "but right from the start, he insisted on calling me by my first name, or, as he pronounced it in his best French, 'Por-leen'."

The couple moved from the shabby Kingston boarding house into Rideau Cottage, a handsome Georgian home on the grounds of Government House. "It was the most lovely house," said Pauline. "And very early every morning, Lord Byng would be out riding on his horse and would pass by and throw pebbles at our window and say 'Come on, lazy Vaniers. Time to get up!'"

The working and living environment at Government House was friendly and stimulating. "However, there were a few pitfalls. For example, my English was not quite on a par with the elegant turns of phrases of British vice-regal entourages, and some of my first efforts at making conversation with distinguished visitors caused much laughter. Such as the time I recommended that a visiting British Lord 'not hesitate to take advantage of the chambermaid,' or said to a Viscountess who had asked me about Lord Byng's cellar, 'Oh, the Governor General's wines leave nothing to hope for!'"

Such innocent errors only helped endear Pauline all the more to the Byngs, and the two couples became lifelong friends. When Georges' tour of duty ended, he was given the singular honour of being invited, at Byng's intervention, to attend the illustrious British Army Staff College in England.

The night before the Vaniers' departure, Lord Byng asked Pauline into his sitting room to reassure her but also warn her of what lay ahead. "Lord Byng said to me, 'As French Canadians in such a bastion of British stuffiness, you will probably be the object of much critical curiosity, and patronized as curious colonials. On the other hand, this might also mean you are invited to meet all sorts of senior people, even perhaps the King and Queen themselves, whom your colleagues will likely never meet. Just make sure that it doesn't go to your head!'

"When he had finished, and it came time to rejoin the others, I was suddenly so distressed by the thought of leaving that I burst into tears. Then he put his arm around my shoulder and walked me back into the living room where he said to the others: 'I fear that dear Por-leen has quite taken the starch out of my shirtfront!'"

Pauline Vanier and her husband, a newly appointed lieutenant-colonel, 1925.

4
Staff College, Camberley, and League of Nations, Geneva (1923-1930)

Pauline was seven months pregnant with her first child when Georges received orders to set sail for England. Neither the prospect of a stormy midwinter Atlantic crossing nor her doctor's dour misgivings could dissuade her from accompanying him. By early January 1923, they arrived safely in the British Army Staff College grounds in Camberley, some 55 kilometres southwest of London.

They registered at the College and were immediately assigned a house called "Balgonie" which came with a maid, a "batman" (orderly) and even a horse for riding to the foxhunt. The Vaniers quickly sought out Georges' fellow army major, Harry Crerar, the only other Canadian enrolled in the two-year military training program. Pauline and his wife, Verse Crerar, had barely set out together to stroll down the High Street when two English army wives passed by, one commenting in a voice fully audible to the Canadians, "Those must be the two little colonials!"

Pauline Vanier at a fancy dress ball in 1927.

"I suspect our leg-wear betrayed us. We wanted to make a good first impression, so had worn our silk stockings and new shoes with daring one-inch-high heels. We soon discovered all our English contemporaries were still in woollen stockings and flat heels!"

Their initial efforts to introduce themselves were politely rebuffed, but Pauline was in time invited to tea to meet some of the other British army wives. "Most of them rather frightened me. One, for example, looked so much like a horse I could hardly believe she was real. When she spoke I almost dropped my teacup — she made a sound just like a horse neighing! I couldn't understand a word she said!"

Pauline noticed one guest, however, with an attractive and sensitive face, so sat down beside her. Assuming she was also a wife of one of the officer students, she said to the woman: "'I'm a bit worried about meeting the instructors' wives: how should I speak to them?' Everyone fell silent. After a pause the woman answered gently, 'Just as you would speak to a student's wife.' Then, when she left the room, everyone broke out in raucous laughter. It seemed I had committed a great faux pas — it turned out I had been speaking to the wife of the Chief Instructor!"

The tea was to be Pauline's only solo encounter with her British counterparts for some time, but she and Georges were both included in an introductory dinner party for all newcomers. "All everyone talked about during the whole dinner was horses, scent, hounds, and drag (the trail of scent left by a fleeing fox). It was all Greek to me and for once I kept silent. This was my introduction to society at the Staff College."

By mid-February, a very pregnant Pauline was turning down most social invitations. And on the 27th of the month, she gave birth to a healthy first child, Thérèse Marie Chérisy Vanier.

Towards the end of their two-year posting and probably through the intervention of Lord Byng, a royal messenger delivered an invitation to the two Vaniers to dine with their Majesties, King George V and Queen Mary, at the Royal Pavillion at Aldershot.

Pauline was by now pregnant again, which made it difficult to find a suitable dress for the occasion. Georges had already bought an old Citroen but felt he should borrow a car more suitable for their grand entrance to the Pavillion grounds.

"When we arrived, we were inspected at the door by a towering lady-in-waiting who was even taller than I. She gave me one look and said that my hair was a mess and sent me off with a maid to comb it.... What an inauspicious beginning."

The Vaniers were ushered into a waiting room and quickly discovered all the other guests were senior British generals with their lorgnette-wielding wives. "There we were, the poor little Vaniers," sighed Pauline. "A fanfare announced Their Majesties' entrance; the men bowed, the ladies curtsied and the guests followed the royal couple into the dining room.

"I was the youngest and least important so I sat at the tail end of the table. But I was still only three places away from the King. I was so nervous I couldn't eat a thing."

Pauline found herself even closer to the Princess Royal, and noted that she seemed to be just as pregnant as she herself was. "I was desperate to make some conversation that might interest her so I said, 'I think you will have a baby about the same age as mine.' 'Yes,' she answered crisply, then turned away and never said another word to me throughout the dinner! I learned later that royal ladies do not usually appear in public if they are expecting a child, but if they do so, any reference to their condition is considered very bad manners indeed!"

After dinner, the ladies withdrew to another room, and were individually taken to Queen Mary for a few private words.

"I was, of course, the last, and when the Queen registered who I was she surreptitiously took a cigarette from her purse and lit it up. But at that precise moment the King and the male guests started arriving to join us. Her Majesty quickly put out the cigarette and jammed the butt into her purse, just like a young schoolgirl caught in the act!"

Upon learning of their dinner with the King and Queen, the Vaniers' colleagues were so impressed that they greeted Georges and Pauline like conquering heroes on their return to the Staff College. "From then on, we were invited out to dinner almost every night for the next three months! Georges was even asked to give a lecture to his fellow students, and succeeded in ensuring that Harry Crerar was given a similar honour."

Georges had completed the Staff College course by the spring of 1925 and was appointed, with the new rank of lieutenant-colonel, to command his old regiment, the Royal 22nd, in Quebec City. So the family returned to Canada and moved into the Citadel, a handsome fortress overlooking the St. Lawrence River. There was a spirited atmosphere among the military families and their life was a busy round of formal dinners and military functions, fancy dress balls and tennis parties.

Later that year, on November 30th, Pauline gave birth again, this time to her first son. "We christened him Georges, but since Lord and Lady Byng had consented to be godparents, we soon nicknamed him 'Byngsie,' a name used by his family and close friends long after he had become Father Benedict of the contemplative order of Trappist monks."

Lord Byng was to complete his term as Governor General the following year, and would no doubt have left Canada as the most popular vice-regent in the young nation's history, had it not been for a tragic confrontation with the Canadian Prime Minister, Mackenzie King. King headed a minority government and feared certain defeat in the House of Commons if a highly critical report were tabled in the House. He therefore asked the Governor General to dissolve Parliament and call elections immediately, before the report could be presented.

Lord Byng believed that an opportunity should first be given to the large Conservative party to try to form a government. Only after the Conservatives' efforts failed did Byng agree to a dissolution and new elections.

Mackenzie King immediately launched a fiery election campaign contending that Byng's initial refusal represented British intrusion in Canadian political affairs. King won the election with a slim majority. Nonetheless, he never softened the extreme position he had taken in his campaign, nor did he seek reconciliation with the Governor General whose reputation he had so unscrupulously sullied. "I don't think Mr. King ever realized how grievously Lord Byng suffered over that incident," said Pauline.

The Vaniers spent that summer's vacation in Murray Bay on the lower St. Lawrence. "The Byngs were frequent visitors and I remember Lord Byng sitting for hours with Georges, constantly reviewing the correctness of his original decision. He also took many long walks with me. Several times a week we'd go out and walk for miles. He wouldn't say a word, just heave big sighs and say, 'Oh me.' I felt that he was a broken-hearted man."

The Byngs left Canada from Quebec City on September 30th. "He left a crushed and ill man, sick with heart disease," said Pauline. He was, however, to live another nine years in Britain, continued to participate in public affairs, and cherished the faithful friendship of the Vaniers to the end.

The Byngs were succeeded by Lord and Lady Willingdon who quickly made the Vaniers' acquaintance by visiting Quebec ("Make sure there are lots of police in evidence," ordered the new Governor General) and, in particular, the Citadel, where they declared the accommodation for vice-regal visitors entirely inadequate. Willingdon did, however, ask Georges to retain his position as honorary aide-de-camp, which meant occasional visits to Ottawa.

"Lady Willingdon was as much a stickler as her husband and was never satisfied with the depth and enthusiasm of my curtsies. On one occasion when my curtsy to her was not as deep as it had been to Lord Willingdon, she bellowed in a loud and demanding voice 'LOWER!'"

On 15 March 1927, a second son arrived and they named him Bernard. Early that summer the family rented a house at Pointe-au-Pic, also on the lower St. Lawrence, where they could spend the vacation with their three children. But tragedy was soon to strike: one night in late June, fire suddenly broke out and consumed the whole building. All the family, as well as Pauline's mother and their nanny, barely escaped the sudden inferno. Everything in the house, however, was lost — clothes, precious papers, and all of Pauline's jewelry, including her wedding ring.

Her family's close brush with death on top of her strenuous social demands had a serious effect on Pauline's health. She began to feel the onset of a nervous breakdown. Experiencing constant headaches and recurring fits of deep depression, she even feared she had a brain tumour. "It was a bad, bad period and I'm ashamed to say it went on for almost seven years."

Hoping that a change might help restore his wife's health and *joie de vivre,* Georges agreed in 1928 to leave his regiment and accept the post of military representative on the Canadian delegation to the League of Nations in Geneva. It turned out, however, that the atmosphere in Geneva was hardly conducive to Pauline's recuperation. The world economic depression was reaching its lowest point and Europe was drifting towards war. Consequently, a feeling of cynicism and despair pervaded both Geneva and the League of Nations.

Worrying, too, was the fact that Georges' entire savings had been wiped out in the stock market crash of 1929.

"He lost all his money and he had debts everywhere. And here we were with three children and a nanny, a young Scottish girl named Isabel Thomson, to support. In fact, both Nanny Thomson and her young niece, Agnes Young, worked for us for two years without pay. Georges was only able to pay them back years later.

"So, alas, I got worse rather than better in Geneva. My weight dropped 20 pounds to a mere 115. And I became quite paranoid. I was afraid of everyone, everything. I went through the rituals of diplomatic entertaining, but neither my heart nor my head was in them. It must have been a dreadful burden for Georges. I know I made him suffer very deeply but he never showed anything. He was so incredibly patient."

All this was made worse by a serious physical illness that required immediate surgery. The aftermath of the operation is recorded in Georges' diary: "(I am allowed) to see Pauline as she is starting to regain consciousness. Her colour is good and clear. She asks, 'Is it all over ... is it really finished?' I assure her that it is. 'Poor Georges — will you put some water on my tongue. Have they cut me up? ... Give me some air, Georges.' A nurse gives her an injection of morphine, and, little by little, as I hold her hand, she goes back to sleep..."

The accumulation of these sufferings and misfortunes overwhelmed Pauline in self-doubt: she doubted her own strength and ability to cope, and she questioned God's willingness to continue to sustain her. She felt useless, unwanted and unmotivated. Her compassion for the suffering of others was exhausted and her Lord, rather than replenishing it with His own love, seemed indifferent. The result was a deep crisis in her spiritual life. "In effect I lost all my faith," she recalled. "It was a time of such great pain — mental, spiritual and physical."

She was also deeply concerned about how to care for her children during this crisis. Luckily, she had her two devoted nannies.

"They developed so many good things in the children. Their love of nature, for example. Nanny Thomson had a practical Scottish turn of mind and great discretion. She would say, 'I'm Presbyterian and does it matter if I say my prayers with the children at night?' I could never have managed without her. She stayed with us for 17 years."

While they were in Geneva, Georges was invited to attend a Naval Conference in London. Pauline had by now learned to type — "very slowly with just two fingers on my own small portable typewriter" — and she often helped Georges with his secretarial work. So when Georges' invitation to London arrived, Pauline was invited along too — as a full member of the delegation.

"No sooner had I arrived at the hotel, joined Georges in our room and began to change than he asked me to take a letter. So there I was, typing away in my dressing gown when the valet came in to deliver some shoes. I knew exactly what I was taken for: I was obviously the typist who was living with the gentleman. His suspicions were confirmed when Georges bent over and gave me an affectionate kiss on the cheek!"

One bright spot during Pauline's stay in Geneva was a visit by Mackenzie King, who, sensitive to their affection for the Byngs, was eager to gain the Vaniers' friendship.

"King was a bachelor, so I was startled when he not only pointed out that he knew I was pregnant again, but announced with great authority that I was going to produce a son. And he was right. I had another boy!" She called her third son Jean, but Georges named him "Jock" in deference to their Scottish nanny; the name is with him still. "Nanny insisted on giving him his bath and calling him 'my wee Jock' right up until he was nine. And long after that, when Jock was in the navy, he'd take Nanny out to the cinema and she'd say to this tall strapping midshipman: 'Now Jock darlin', give me your hand to cross the street.'"

Lord Byng sent his congratulations on the arrival of her fourth child and added a mischievous aside for Pauline: "Could it be possible you're thinking of starting a little League of Nations of your own?"

The Vaniers made many enduring friends in that period. One was Agnes Macphail, the first woman elected to the Canadian Parliament. She was appointed to the Canadian delegation to the League of Nations where, as a militant pacifist, she insisted on serving on the disarmament committee with a secret determination to have all armies permanently abolished.

"Imagine her dismay when she learned that Georges Vanier was being assigned to work with her. I think she arrived in Geneva convinced any professional soldier would greet her with blood still on his hands and a sword buckled permanently at his side.

"I wasn't sure Georges' no-nonsense pragmatism would leave much space for what he would surely consider Agnes' irrational pacifism, so before her arrival I discussed her point of view with him at length. He seemed impressed by my interpretations. Happily, in less than a week, we had won agreement on a compromise position, and we became fast friends.

"A colleague on the French delegation, Colonel Réquin, was so surprised by Agnes' transformation that, at one of our meetings, he mischievously drew a comical sketch of Georges leading Agnes around Geneva like a pet poodle!"

On another occasion, when Agnes came down with the flu, Georges said he planned to take her flowers, but suggested that Pauline might like to call in person as well. "I arrived at her hotel and was told by the concierge, a little man with a black drop coat, that under no circumstances could she be disturbed. 'Nonsense,' I said, and marched up to her room, the concierge following sheepishly behind. Just as I approached the door, I heard Georges' voice inside. It suddenly dawned on me that the concierge was protecting Georges and Agnes McPhail!

"My, there were a lot of first-rate women who came over to Geneva at that time. But Agnes was the pick of the bunch."

The Vanier family aboard ship, 1938. From left to right: Pauline, Thérèse, Bernard, Jean, Byngsie, Georges.

5
Canada House, London (1931-1938)

Prime Minister R.B. Bennett was anxious to strengthen the Canadian High Commission in London, so he persuaded Georges Vanier to accept a diplomatic appointment as "Secretary," or assistant to the High Commissioner, Howard Ferguson. Thus in April 1931, the family moved from Geneva into a handsome Regency house on Regent's Park in London.

"It was much too extravagant for our battered resources. Georges never told me about our financial difficulties until much later when I discovered that he had the distinction of being overdrawn in each of the six main Canadian banks!"

Pauline was still weak during their first months in London and on some days she hardly left her bed. "It was a bad, bad time for me," she recalled. "I was in and out of bed for three months, worrying about everything, specially the fact that we might have to send the three boys to boarding school. I just couldn't accept the idea of parting with them. Yes, I not only behaved very badly. I was thoroughly impossible."

But at least the period was intellectually invigorating. "I began reading again. Georges shared with me some of his favourite literature, especially the English classics; I enjoyed Jane Austen and William Makepeace Thackeray the best because they poke such fun at the pretensions of English country gentry. I also came to love English poetry, and found in it great spiritual consolation and immense beauty. I think these books did more than anything else to lift me out of my long struggle with self-doubt and depression."

One of the first fruits of this emergence was her insistence that they abandon "one of our own pretensions," the Regent's Park mansion, and move into a modest row house in Oxford Square. "It did wonders for my figure: it was all up and down, four floors with only one room of any size on each floor." To help pay off Georges' overdrafts, Pauline sold all her jewelry and replaced it with imitations.

They managed to send the three boys to a private prep day school, one whose sole purpose was to prepare them for the elitist upper grade "public" school, Winchester. "When the time came to tell the headmaster that the school we had in mind for the boys was not Winchester but a Catholic school called Beaumont College, he exploded in anger and almost threw me out on my ear. He felt the two years he had spent teaching them were entirely wasted."

Pauline eventually recovered from her illness and could once again help Georges with the social and sometimes technical aspects of his duties. She was recruited to help organize an international conference on naval matters and invited with the rest of the Canadian delegation to a lunch at 10 Downing Street with the then British Prime Minister, Ramsay MacDonald.

"As the only woman invited, I found myself seated at his right hand. Imagine my dismay, and even greater disillusion, to discover that this revered leader, though barely 70, was already practically senile. He could not grasp what the conference was about, who we were, or much less what countries we came from.

"Most of the conversation was quite incoherent, although he took delight in recounting the time he entertained the sharp-tongued British politician, Nancy Astor. What he remembered most about the occasion, he told me, was when she whispered huskily in his ear: 'You may think I'm attractive but the best part of me is under the table!' And this was the Prime Minister of Britain!"

There was another rude surprise at that lunch. "The meal consisted of aged mutton and cabbage, both boiled until they were gray, followed by a dessert of equally gray unflavoured junket. We all pretended we had to leave early so we could get a decent meal in a nearby restaurant and be back in time for the afternoon session!"

Pauline, eager to find an outlet for her newly re-stored energy, contacted Maurice Cassidy, her doctor. "They suspected a dysfunctional heart, but it didn't stop me from asking if I could join him on his hospital rounds, to help bring cheer and encouragement to some of the lonelier patients. We visited everyone in two of the men's wards. And afterwards, Cass said to me, 'You have a very real gift with the sick. Would you consider coming on a regular basis? You could do so much good.' I was thrilled with his suggestion and I arranged to spend at least one afternoon a week in the wards.

"For me it was the most stimulating experience. I came to know every possible kind of Englishman: coal miners, music hall performers, garbage collectors, tram drivers. In all, I continued these visits for almost eight years."

Pauline kept in touch with many of those patients or their families for years afterwards. "One of my favourites was young Billy Marshall. He'd begun at 12 working in the mines and, by 18, his lungs had become clogged from the dust he inhaled all day and he devel-oped silicosis. There was no known cure for this ailment, so after several months of steady decline they decided as a last hope to remove a lung. The operation was described as a success, but Billy died soon after."

Some time later, the hospital received a letter addressed simply to "The Madame" of the ward: it was from the boy's mother to Pauline. "It was a letter of such great beauty. From then on, that woman wrote to me twice a year without fail, and when war broke out she wrote at once from her home in Gloucester offering to look after our children until the war was over. 'They'd be perfectly safe in our village,' she assured me, 'and there'll be no shortage of food since we're surrounded by farms. It would be such a privilege for us!'

"We didn't take up her offer, because we were soon sent back to Canada ourselves. But I kept corresponding with her right up until we were at Government House. After she passed away in the 1960s, her daughter found all my letters wrapped up in tissue paper and tied together with a mauve ribbon. She sent the bundle to me in gratitude."

It was at this time that the Vaniers came to know the English writer, Rudyard Kipling, author of such popular yarns as *The Jungle Book* and *Captains Courageous*. "We found him such a warm-hearted, wise and imaginative person with a wonderful empathy for children. We once said to him, 'We have a son who says you know how to make jungle noises.' So Mr. Kipling immediately sent a personal note addressed to 'The boy who says I know how to make jungle noises.' By the time Byngsie had written to thank him, I saw in the paper that he had died.

"Georges paid him a warm tribute soon after when he said: 'Few writers have been able to write for children and for men. Kipling was able to do this.... Anyone who has known him or read his books is the better for it.'"

In 1936, Vincent Massey arrived to take over as High Commissioner for Canada in London. He was joined by Mike and Maryon Pearson and the Vaniers soon became close friends with all three.

"It was the time of the abdication of Edward VIII and what dramatic days those were. Maryon and I would always go down to the Caledonian market to buy our vegetables. We both loved our outings there and those wonderful cockneys who call you 'dearie' and 'darlin.'

"We went down the day after the abdication speech, and the men who sold potatoes were all wearing black ties. 'We're in mourning for our liberty,' they told us. 'But why,' we asked. 'Because of what he did. He chose the woman he loved instead of choosing us!' There were many who said the people of England supported Edward because of his romance; well, that just wasn't true.

"The couple left for Austria that night and I remember how we listened so intensely to every news bulletin. Prime Minister Baldwin broadcast first, then (Winston) Churchill. Then we waited for the reactions from the Dominions and when they came in, most of them were against it. They just didn't accept Mrs. Simpson.

"Then things cooled down a little and before we knew it, we were celebrating the coronation of King George VI. Those were such exciting times. I wouldn't have missed them for anything."

Before leaving London, Pauline's unrelenting compassion helped bring about a profound change in Georges Vanier's spiritual orientation. Georges had long been proud of the firmness of his faith and of his almost military-like sense of duty to his Creator. Like the writer Ernest Psichari and the Jansenist theologians of the seventeenth and eighteenth centuries, Georges believed that a Christian should put the quest for personal holiness, unquestioning obedience, and self-discipline at the top of his or her ambitions. Any projection of love was thus a lower priority.

But this order of precedence changed completely after hearing one sermon. It was given by a Scottish priest, Father R.H.J. Steuart, in the spring of 1938. Pauline had always been impressed by the Jesuit priest's quiet wisdom and humanity and it was on her urging that her husband attended the Good Friday service with her.

Father Steuart declared that the transcendent quality of God is not so much majesty as love: a love for all God's creation, a love God invites all humankind to share and to reflect to those around them. While this love for others had always inspired Pauline, from that day on, it inspired Georges as well.

Georges' change in spiritual orientation helped draw the couple closer together. While Georges had always written to Pauline every day whenever they were apart, and consistently showed her the greatest affection, he hesitated to reveal the deeper secrets of his mind to her. As Robert Speaight wrote in his biography of Georges Vanier: "Where she (Pauline) was extroverted and communicative, he was naturally reserved. She had his heart, but she would have liked to have more of his mind — as much as she was eager to give him of her own. Suddenly, however, under the influence of Father Steuart's meditation, the barrier was removed. Henceforward, she was able to speak, and he to listen. In his more reflective, less impulsive, way, he spoke as well. He had always been a rock on which she could rely, and now the hidden springs within it were released to their mutual enrichment."

That summer, the Vaniers left London for Canada, not realizing at the time that an even more challenging posting in Europe lay ahead.

6
Paris on the Eve of War
(1939-1940)

In December 1938, Mackenzie King offered Georges Vanier the position of Minister and head of mission at the Canadian legation in Paris. Though a legation is a rank below an embassy, Georges Vanier would soon wield more influence — and carry more prestige — than most ambassadors in Paris.

The French bureaucracy, however, only gradually recognized the stature of the new Canadian representative. On the first day Georges and Pauline arrived in January 1939, Pauline consulted the Chief of Protocol in the French foreign ministry to determine whom she should visit to pay her respects. Normally, the wife of a new ambassador called on the wives of the French Prime Minister and Foreign Minister as well as those of other notables and diplomats.

"The Chief of Protocol turned out to be a woman — and an enormously fat one at that," Pauline noted. "I was very frightened and asked her whom I should call on. Obviously she was unable to conceive of Canada as an independent country, viewing it rather as some sort of American puppet or appendage. She flatly turned down the idea of the wife of a representative from what she saw as a non-country having any right to call on anyone at all. Only after I'd pressed her did she suggest that 'Well, I suppose you *could* call on the *American* ambassador's wife.'"

The American ambassador, Bill Bullitt, had been in Paris longer than any other ambassador and was therefore unofficial dean of the diplomatic corps. Both he and his wife received Pauline immediately. "She cheered me up by telling me that when she first arrived here protocol didn't know what to do with her either; she was born in Brazil, and they couldn't imagine how a Brazilian could represent the United States. So they used to refer to her husband, at least for diplomatic purposes, as being single!

"'But we'll fix them!', she said, and promptly arranged for me to come as her guest to a major women's conference in Paris, to which were invited the wives of many senior French government ministers and of all the other ambassadors in town. She saw that I met and talked with every one of importance I needed to and from then on I was treated as the wife of a senior and important ambassador.

"But oh, I was so lost among all those ambassadors' wives. I didn't know how to behave, when to sit and stand. I guess I learned quickly enough."

The Vaniers' launching on the Parisian social scene, however, was rudely interrupted by a near tragedy. "Our first major reception was for the papal delegate and we were pleased to receive acceptances from senior church officials (including two cardinals), from government and diplomatic circles, and from several leading figures in literary and academic circles. I was so anxious that everything go well, and was counting on Georges' serene and commanding presence to calm my nervousness.

"Georges was planning to take the afternoon off to help me prepare. But at 11:30 that morning, he called to say he was leaving for the airport at once to catch a flight for London. He had just received a call from Byngsie's school near Windsor and learned that our son was seriously ill and might need an immediate operation. Georges had no time to explain; he told me later that when he had heard of Byngsie's condition, the reception simply vanished from his mind.

"Of course I stayed on to run the reception — there was no way I could call off such a large number of guests — but I was sick with worry not knowing what was wrong with Byngsie. I can hardly remember what happened during the gathering: I must have appeared terribly distracted, but many of our guests later gallantly referred to the event as one of the most successful they had been to in Paris."

Pauline heard nothing from London until late that evening, and the news was alarming. "Byngsie had a ruptured appendix and did indeed need an immediate operation. The whole of his intestinal cavity was badly infected and he was in a coma. This was before the days of antibiotics, and the chances of survival seemed slim.

"The next morning, I booked the first plane to London. Georges met me and took me straight to the hospital. 'I'll be honest with you,' Byngsie's doctor told us, 'if it were not for his youth, I would say he had no chance. But since he's only 13, there may be some hope.' Father Lillie, the rector of Byngsie's college, had joined us at the hospital and tried to prepare me for the worst. 'You must accept the will of God, whatever it is,' he declared. 'I won't,' I shouted. 'He must live!'

"I can still see Father Lillie's reaction: he took from his pocket a small black case with the holy ointments for administering Last Rites, and unclasped his rosary from his belt. 'You must commit him body and soul to the will of God,' he continued. He was telling me that Byngsie was probably going to die, and I had to let him go. The realization hit me like a slap in the face. 'Then take him!' I cried, 'take him alive or dead!'"

Byngsie did not die that second day. "A Mass was held for him at the College and every boy in the school turned out and prayed for him. Then, just as we were leaving the chapel, a call came from the doctor to say Byngsie had been saved. The peritonitis (inflammation of the abdominal membrane) from his ruptured appendix had formed an abscess the size of a small melon inside the abdominal wall. Had the abscess ruptured within the wall, Byngsie would have died. But doctors had been able, almost miraculously, to reach the abscess through the wall and induce it to discharge outside the cavity.

"It took him several weeks before he got back on his feet, but he was saved. I think you could call this a small miracle. From that day on, Georges and I felt that Byngsie would receive a special calling from God. Byngsie, too, must have felt, however vaguely, a similar premonition, for during his convalescence he used to ask for a priest in the middle of the night, and the good Irish Father Tomey would come to him, sometimes at 2:00 in the morning.

"Years later he told us that he felt a call to join the contemplative order of Trappist monks. He suspected we would be surprised and might even oppose his choice. How wrong he was! It was then that I recounted to him the story of his brush with death in London, and of my commitment of him to God's will 'alive or dead.'

"His choice of career has been a good investment! What a rock he was to me many years later when I found my own faith wavering in self-doubt..."

In the summer of 1939, a vast sense of foreboding fell, not only upon France, but upon the entire European continent. Germany was obviously preparing to launch a major war and the mood in Paris became heavy with gloom. Families began hoarding supplies, a sombre military presence set in, and the usually animated Parisian cafe life became muted and melancholy. The Vanier family decided to escape the stifling atmosphere for a short summer holiday in Varengeville, a seaside resort in northern France near Dieppe.

It was to be their last happy time together as a family for several long years. The same proved true for many of their fellow guests at the resort. American film star Bette Davis was there, as was A.P. Herbert, whose comic contributions to the British humour magazine *Punch* had kept the Vaniers laughing for years. With his huge head of curly hair, outsized spectacles, and long, bony, and perpetually bare feet (to help him, he said, type his footnotes), he provided a tremendous boost to their spirits.

"We were trying to forget the impending war so we went out to lunch at a restaurant outside Dieppe. We all ate and drank too much but at the end of lunch A.P. pressed yet one more calvados upon me. I told him that if I drank it, he'd have to carry me out. 'Why, I'd adore the opportunity!' he protested. So I knocked it back, and lo and behold, I found myself too unstable to stand. He was in little better shape himself, but cheerfully threw me over his shoulder and lurched all the way back to the hotel, to the cheers of family, friends, and astonished townsfolk. That was to be the last time we really laughed for five years."

The next day, the French government ordered a general mobilization of all French armed forces. The hotel emptied, experimental curfews and blackouts began and wailing air-raid sirens could be heard at all hours. In addition, ration books were readied for use and movement around the country became difficult. Georges returned at once to Paris, while Pauline and the children stayed on in Varengeville.

Diplomatic dependents had been warned to leave Paris in anticipation of German bombing, so Georges began looking for accommodation for his family in the countryside. It proved a herculean task, for French homeowners in rural areas were giving preference to family and friends over strangers. Finally, a cousin of

Pauline's came to the rescue and remembered that a cousin of her own, a marquis, owned a chateau in a village in Loir-et-Cher, some 200 kilometres southwest of Paris. He readily agreed to take them in. "I think he was happy to have us living there since he feared his chateau might be requisitioned by the French army. He naively assumed that sheltering diplomatic dependents would provide his chateau with diplomatic immunity against requisition."

Arrangements were made just in time, for dependents of all diplomats were soon formally ordered to leave Paris. Georges sent a car with his chauffeur, Joseph, to collect Pauline and the children, who were still on holiday from school, and they all set out for the chateau. The car broke down on the way, but the chauffeur, with a determination born of a desperate fear of the Germans (even though France was not yet officially at war), achieved wonders in repairing it.

It was after sunset by the time the party finally reached the region. "The village was in complete darkness when we arrived and no one answered when the chauffeur knocked on doors seeking directions to the chateau. It was almost midnight before we found the spot, a bleak, somewhat decrepit Louis XIII-style country chateau. A grim-faced marquis met us, and an even grimmer-faced housekeeper showed us to our rooms. 'You are going to be very unhappy here,' she announced solemnly.

"The atmosphere of that place was dreadful," Pauline recalled. "The housekeeper seemed to resent our presence from the start, began stealing from the marquis, and managed to convince him that the Vanier children were to blame. The gardener also hated having the children there and claimed they were to blame for every head of livestock that died or fell ill. When Jock found a calf strangled in the barn and reported it to the gardener, he accused him of the deed. It was one disaster after another. Every time poor Georges came down from Paris on the weekend, he'd find one more catastrophe to cope with."

On September 1, 1939, the Germans invaded Poland; two days later, Poland's guarantors, France and Britain, declared war on Germany. Everyone's worst fears were realized.

After the sudden and brutal German bombing of Polish cities in September, thousands of Parisians anticipated the same demoralizing fate for their city and poured out of Paris to seek refuge in the countryside. They jammed the roads and trains, landing on the doorsteps of astonished and long-forgotten relatives with mattresses, bulging suitcases and bewildered children in tow.

Not anticipating so early an entry into the war on France and Britain's part, however, the Germans were hardly prepared to attack France immediately and a long period of stand-off or "phony war" set in. The refugees warily moved back into Paris and the anxious waiting began.

Meanwhile the Russians, unwilling to see the whole of Poland occupied by Germany, made a deal with Hitler allowing them to annex the eastern third of the country. Their complicity with Germany prompted the French to suspect the loyalty of French communists. Their civil liberties were suspended; the men were imprisoned or conscripted for front-line service and their wives and children were forcibly removed from Paris, where it was felt they might sabotage the French war effort.

Fifty of these communist dependents were trucked to the marquis' village and, because no one would accommodate them, were put up by town officials in ruined or abandoned buildings in the most wretched living conditions. "The treatment of these innocent unfortunates was barbarous. We were determined to help out where we could: I organized relief supplies and better housing, 16-year-old Thérèse organized school classes for the children, while the three boys helped build shelters. My mother had also joined us from Paris so she and I gave them religious instruction and catechism. Then we had all the children baptized!"

Autumn turned to winter without the "phony war" becoming a real one. For no apparent reason the country suffered the same shortages and uncertainties, disruptions in education and social services, as if the Germans had actually invaded.

"Georges became increasingly dismayed with the conditions we were living under. Finally, in April 1940, after almost eight dismal months in the chateau, he found a good excuse for bringing us back to Paris: typhoid had broken out in the village, and he argued with French authorities that, until the Germans actually invaded France, we would be in less danger in Paris than in the countryside. We'd been there eight months and that was enough. So off we went, thank God."

They returned to Paris with some trepidation, and settled back into the Vanier apartment. Pauline was quick to resume her valued role as helpmate to Georges. Indeed, so closely did she become associated with his activities that when the French General Réquin, who was then commanding the French Fifth Army, had asked Georges to visit him on the Maginot Line of French fortifications on the border with Germany, he had invited Pauline along too. "It was the first time such an honour had been given to a woman," she said.

It was a sobering visit. Pauline found herself scrambling over embankments, groping her way through dimly-lit tunnels, and inspecting forward positions. "We were taken right up to the front and we stood just two miles away from the German lines. You couldn't help but think that one well-aimed German artillery shell could have wiped out all of us in a split second.

Though it was still the 'phony war,' the Germans would fire the occasional round, just to let the French know they were there!"

How long would this "phony war" continue? "On the evening of May 9, 1940, the American ambassador, William Bullitt, and his wife invited us to dinner. It was an incredible dinner party: there was such an impressive list of guests: Edouard Daladier, the recently elected French Prime Minister, several other French ministers, and the British air vice-marshal, Barratt." Most wives had been sent to the countryside, so Pauline and the American journalist Dorothy Thompson were among the very few women guests.

"Discussions that evening were intense and rumours were rife. Then, as the evening progressed, footmen stepped forward to whisper messages to one guest after the other, each of whom immediately slipped away. By midnight we found we were the last ones left. We had already suspected what was happening. As Georges and I sat there, the American ambassador confirmed the news that had been passed to the others. By cover of darkness, the Germans had launched an all-out invasion, not only of France but of Belgium and the Netherlands as well.

"We returned home with heavy hearts. I had known that such an invasion was inevitable, but now that it had started we all felt sick to our stomachs.

"None of us got much sleep that night. About 4:00 a.m., air raid sirens began shrieking on every side. We got the children up and dressed and we retreated to our makeshift shelter in the cellar. There we sat while Paris was being subjected to its first attack from the air. This was it. We were at war."

7
Escape from France
(May - June 1940)

That air attack was enough for Georges. "When he left for the legation the next morning, he told me to pack a small suitcase for mother and each of the children and stay by the telephone. Not long after he called and said brusquely: 'Don't ask any questions. The car is coming to pick you up and he knows where to take you. God bless you. Good bye.'

"Almost at once, the legation chauffeur was at the door, with instructions to take us all to a countryside retreat, though he was not told to whom it belonged. Our destination was a mystery to us although I knew it was somewhere along the road to Blois and Bordeaux to the south. Already there were German planes overhead, sirens were screaming, and the roads were quickly becoming jammed with refugees shuffling along in never-ending columns.

"It took us the rest of the day to travel less than 200 kilometres. We followed Georges' directions and finally turned down a side road that led to a tiny cottage. An elderly gentleman opened the door and identified himself as a Mr. Walker. He said he knew someone at the Canadian legation; it was not Georges but of course we would be most welcome. There were beds for me and my mother, but the four children had to sleep on the floor, which they thought was huge fun. Meanwhile, Joseph, our long-suffering chauffeur, wearily drove off into the night to try to get back to Paris.

"We stayed there several days, long enough for Jock to come down with a serious ear infection. In fact, it looked so bad that I was afraid it might cost him his hearing in that ear. But all doctors in the area had been conscripted into the army. Again what good providence: a doctor fleeing Paris stopped to ask directions, and he agreed to drain Jock's abscess and thus save his hearing. So all was well."

But their supposedly safe haven was not safe for long. The house where they were staying lay between the Loire river, with its heavy shipping traffic, and the main railway line from Paris to Bordeaux; both were prime targets in what was proving to be the main German aerial objective — to cripple the French transportation network.

"Tension and fear were everywhere. At night there were inexplicable flashing lights apparently directed at German aircraft overhead, and local people believed a vast 'fifth column' of German spies and sympathizers was everywhere. The roads became jammed with fleeing refugees. At first they were mostly in cars and motorcycles, but as gasoline became scarce, the endless queues were now comprised of carts and bicycles. We set up a stand by the highway and offered the most urgent cases coffee and whatever meagre provisions we could lay our hands on.

"Many of the refugees were a pathetic sight. One old man arrived with a worn-out horse hauling a wagonload of hay. He explained that it was all he had left of any value. His house and farm had been put to the torch by the Germans, and his entire family had been killed during an artillery bombardment.

"Another cart was driven by a woman in her eighties and held three very young children and their remaining possessions, including a sheep and some hens. I offered her some coffee, then asked her where she had come from and why she had left. She looked at me and said, 'Madame, we could do nothing else.' She came from a village near Lille, near the Belgian border and directly on the line of what turned out to be the main German advance. 'My house, my whole village, was destroyed by German tanks,' she said. 'My grandsons were in the fields and the Germans seized them and took them off for forced labour; their wives were raped by German soldiers and then taken away — my neighbours said they would be placed in a brothel. These babies are my great grandchildren, and these possessions are all that we have left.'"

The German *blitzkrieg* was carrying all before it, and Georges soon realized his family's "safe haven" was in fact a likely target for German bombers. He managed to reach Pauline by phone and told her to take the children by whatever means possible to friends in the countryside to the west, still north of the Loire. There, they would be closer to Bordeaux, the last port from which they could escape by sea if, as now seemed certain, France fell.

Pauline walked to Blois, found a firm willing to rent her a car and chauffeur and returned to the Walker cottage to collect the family. "We had already loaded the car when suddenly a premonition came over me. I said to the children, 'Get out, we're not leaving.' 'But Mummy,' Thérèse protested, 'you promised Daddy we would!' I could not understand why I had this sudden conviction that we should not follow Georges' instructions. So we unloaded the car and sent the driver off.

"The bombing increased that night, and I thought I must have made a mistake. I suddenly remembered I had cousins who lived to the south, across the Loire. I was able to reach them by phone, and they came at once and collected us. I shall never forget the look on the faces of the people in the village when they saw us go.

They knew that if we were leaving, France must be doomed."

That night the German planes came over in waves in a massive attack on communication links, and succeeded in destroying every bridge across the Loire from Blois to the sea. "Had we gone to the west the day before, we would certainly have been cut off from escape to the south and stuck there for the rest of the war. Worse still, we could have been discovered by the Germans and imprisoned. Say what you will, we were jolly lucky."

As it was, her hosts learned that the Germans had encircled Paris and would probably overrun the southwest of France within days. Pauline managed to contact Georges. "Your premonition was correct and your hosts are right," he replied. "Don't budge. I will be there as soon as possible."

In fact, the Germans began their assault on Paris that same afternoon. "Georges closed and sealed the legation, and was the last foreign diplomat to leave, evading the German advance forces and escaping from the city a half hour before midnight. It was a terrible trip, with machine gunning all along the road. The journey to Blois, which would normally take three hours, took them almost 17. Georges brought with him the last legation secretary, as well as Joseph, the Polish-Jewish chauffeur and his wife, and their bewildered cat."

Georges felt compelled to stop and look for the other members of the legation fleeing Paris, so he sent Pauline and the children on their way south almost immediately. "All he said to me was, 'A car is coming for you. Leave at once. I hope I shall see you soon. God bless you.'

"There was panic all around us. They were already putting straw barricades on the roads and sticks in the fields to prevent parachutists from landing. A group of French airmen walking south lined the roads, their faces distraught as they glanced into our car. And all the time the Germans were flying overhead. A German Messerschmitt fighter crashed right in front of us so I got out and climbed into a ditch close enough to the pilot to see his swastika. I wanted to see whether he had survived. He had not.

"We were nearing Poitiers, still 200 kilometres short of Bordeaux, when we exhausted our last jerry can of gasoline, and the car came to a sickly halt. I could see a gas station a short way ahead and sent Joseph off to see if they had any fuel left. He came back crestfallen. 'It is closed for the duration,' he reported, 'and people I met told me there is no gasoline anywhere between here and Bordeaux.'

"I told the children to get out their rosaries, and we prayed for guidance. Then I asked Joseph to go back and keep knocking on the door until he got an answer. He did, and after ten minutes a man appeared and eventually said he would give us his last jerry can of gasoline. It was enough to get us to Bordeaux."

At long last, the weary travellers inched their way into Bordeaux, only to find that it was bereft of lodging and overrun by refugees. So they pushed on toward the sea, stopping at the village of Cantenac.

"We arrived about 6:00 p.m. and were welcomed royally by the mayor, such a nice little man who invited us to stay with him. It was marvellous. As most of the villagers had already fled, the remaining inhabitants had swept out the abandoned houses, put straw on the floors, clean sheets on the beds, and a bottle of Bordeaux wine and a loaf of bread in each kitchen. All this was done so the town could welcome refugees."

Georges managed to find Pauline and the family at 1:00 a.m. that night. Disturbing rumours were already circulating that the French government was contemplating the unthinkable, an armistice with its German conquerors. Georges and Pauline reluctantly decided they should be ready to leave on a moment's notice.

Merchant ships at the small seaport of Le Verdon at the mouth of the Gironde River were ordered not to leave without taking on refugees. A British destroyer was sent up the Gironde to Bordeaux to pick up shiploads of passengers and transfer them to the merchant ships.

Women and children were to be taken first. "I knew there wasn't a minute to lose but when I saw they were taking women and children first, I made a scene and declared I wouldn't go without Georges. Then other wives began to do the same until an English officer said to me: 'Madame Vanier, you are the senior woman, so you must set an example.' I felt ashamed of my selfishness, so we boarded at once. There on the deck was a little group of English nuns — the Holy Child nuns, all looking quite terrified. I was, too, but tried hard to appear confident. So we all stood silently praying together as the boat slipped away after dark."

In Le Verdon, the destroyer tied up beside the cargo ship *Nariva*, redirected from its usual duties of carrying beef from Argentina, and the 200 women and children refugees scrambled up the rope ladders onto the larger ship. The captain had decided it would be safer to set off by daylight, because the German bombers had previously been attacking coastal shipping by night.

"It might in fact have been better to leave that night because the German bombers came over in hordes and were concentrating on land targets rather than shipping. We were close to land, and the noise was terrifying. Fortunately, we were below deck, all of us crowded into a small cabin near the bridge, with one bunk for me and the boys and another for Thérèse and my mother. We all had our rosaries around our necks when the bombing started. Luckily, the children could not see the explosions or know how close they were. Still, I was afraid they would catch my own fear, which it was difficult to hide.

"Just when the real bombing was underway, a friendly ship's officer who introduced himself as Ralph

Tedman came in. He said he was checking that everyone was wearing their life jackets, but when he realized how scared my children were, not to mention their mother, he sat down on the floor, and, for about two hours, told us the most wonderful stories to take our minds off the bombing.

"We saw him several times again during the voyage and later he came to see us on a number of occasions in London. He obviously loved the children and would take them to the zoo or to the movies. One day, I asked him why he had been so kind to the children and he explained that his own childhood had been very sad so he left home at 16. 'I found in your children something so pure,' he told me. 'I was enchanted to be with them.' Then, when we said goodbye, he opened his shirt and showed me a big silver cross hanging around his neck. 'I'm not a Catholic but this was given to me by a priest in South America and, ever since I've worn it, some of the most wonderful and unexplainable things have happened to me — like meeting you and your children. You will never know how much this meeting has meant to me.'

"So back to our voyage. By next morning, there was still no sign of Georges. We learned that another load of refugees had been taken on board, and every inch of deck space was occupied by sleeping servicemen. They were British airmen whose planes had been destroyed on the ground at an airport at Tours. They had marched non-stop for 48 hours.

"Our ship was crammed to overflowing, so rations were tightly controlled. By the end of the first day, we were already restricted to two salmon paste sandwiches a day and tea made with salt sea water. To pass the time, the children counted the lifeboats on the ship, multiplied by the number of people each one could hold without capsizing, and announced cheerfully that if the ship sank at least 300 of us would have to swim the rest of the way!

"The next morning I was up at 5:00 a.m. and went up on deck. It was a beautiful, clear morning and I saw a German plane flying low overhead. It dropped something that looked like a black umbrella — a spherical object that splashed into the water directly in front of us. The captain immediately put the engines in full reverse, which shook us to pieces, but succeeded in swinging the vessel abruptly to the right.

"At first none of the ship's crew let on that anything serious had happened. Only much later did one of them admit that it was a magnetic mine. It was designed to anchor itself beneath the surface and explode when a ship crosses above it. The captain told me later that we probably hadn't been able to avoid crossing above it, in spite of our violent swerving away from it. The fact that it didn't explode was probably because there hadn't been enough time for it to anchor itself to the sea bottom."

The next morning, at dawn, an escort finally came out to meet the ship and together they zigzagged their way north. What would normally have been a one-day trip became a five-day ordeal, with abrupt changes of course to make the ship harder for German submarines to torpedo.

They headed first for Falmouth in the southwest of England, but were waved off in the nick of time by a British destroyer just as they were about to enter a minefield sewn by German bombers. The passengers were not informed of the minefield as the ship headed back out to sea. Only in the middle of the night did the captain feel confident enough to tell them he hoped to dock the ship next day at Milford Haven.

"That was the most incredible journey. When we arrived in Milford Haven, we noticed that the captain looked terribly haggard and completely wrung out. We learned later that the poor man, unable to handle so much stress, had committed suicide soon after. It was poor Tedman who found him on the bridge, shot through the head.

"What a great feeling it was at last to dock at Milford Haven. We were welcomed by Red Cross volunteers with sweets, baskets of fruit, and advances of money. 'Thank God to be back on English soil,' cried one passenger. 'Look you, this is not England at all!' replied a volunteer sharply. 'This is Wales!'

"My first thought was to phone London to ask about Georges' fate. There was no news, but Vincent Massey told us to take the first train to London. We did, and both Lillian and Vincent Massey were at the station to greet us, with nightgowns and pyjamas and a tooth brush for each of us. We had brought with us only the clothes we were wearing and were so dirty and bedraggled that at first the Park Lane Hotel hesitated to let us in!"

Pauline learned the next day that Georges had stayed in Bordeaux until the last possible moment, in hopes that he and his colleagues could help put some spine in the French resistance. It was to no avail. The new French government signed a humiliating armistice with the Germans, whose terms included immediate German occupation of France's entire Atlantic coast.

With all evacuation ships having left Le Verdon, Georges and two British colleagues were forced to flee to the village of Arcachon, on the coast west of Bordeaux. There they commissioned the skipper of a small sardine fishing boat called *Le Cygne* (The Swan) to take them to sea the next morning. They set out at daybreak in a violent storm and the vessel pitched and tossed as the captain fought to avoid capsizing. "Never have I seen a boat less like a swan," Georges would joke much later.

Suddenly, through the driving rain, the gray-blue outline of a warship appeared. Seeing the fishing boat's distress, the warship turned in front of the vessel to shelter the smaller ship from the wind. Georges, able to use only his one good leg, hauled himself up the rope ladder to reach the warship's deck. To his amazement, the man who greeted him at the top of the ladder was an old friend and former comrade-in-arms, Wallace Creery. The two looked at each other in astonishment, and cried out almost in unison, "What on earth are *you* doing *here*!"

Creery's answer was simple: the warship was the Canadian destroyer *HMCS Fraser* and Creery was its captain. Georges and his colleagues were treated to the most generous hospitality. To speed their arrival to England, however, Creery arranged to transfer them to the British cruiser *HMS Galatea,* which was heading for Plymouth. The *Galatea* docked in Plymouth the following day, and Georges arrived in London that evening, to be greeted by a much relieved Pauline.

The *Fraser* continued on patrol in the Bay of Biscay, but, tragically, was sunk two days later. To the Vanier's relief, most of the crew were rescued, including the unquenchable Wallace Creery, who went on to command other Canadian warships with great distinction.

8
Wartime London
(June - September 1940)

The Vaniers faced a rocky start in London. Obliged to abandon all their possessions in Paris, they arrived in Britain with just the clothes on their backs — no personal belongings, no furniture, and almost no financial resources. They therefore, at first, had to rely entirely on the hospitality of friends. "Imagine our good fortune when an American friend sent me a cable from New York with an offer we couldn't refuse: the use of her flat in Grosvenor Square, fully furnished, plus the services of a butler and a stock of champagne in the fridge."

British authorities anticipated heavy bombing of the city, and therefore strongly recommended that children be evacuated. The Vaniers reluctantly decided to send their four to Canada, together with Pauline's intrepid mother, on a Polish ship travelling by convoy. "How my heart ached to see them go," she recalled. "I was told much later that friends of ours heard that the vessel had been sunk, but thank God they didn't tell us. It wasn't true and the ship reached Canada safely."

London, by this time, was a strange mixture of excitement and foreboding. Legions of European refugees had managed to make their way to England and many of them were anxious to contribute to the British war effort and the liberation of their countries. The British for their part could only hope and pray that their underequipped air force could resist the anticipated German bomber attacks.

Georges settled in at Canada House, the Canadian High Commission in Trafalgar Square. In France, the war-time premier, Paul Reynaud, had handed over the reins of government to the World War I hero, Maréchal Philippe Pétain, who was now 84. On June 16, to the dismay of most Frenchmen, Pétain had signed the armistice with the Germans which allowed them to occupy two-thirds of the country. The remaining third was allowed to set up its own government headquartered in the small town of Vichy, with Pétain as "head of state."

Georges Vanier was still officially the Canadian Minister to France, but in Canadian eyes this meant to Vichy France under Pétain. The Maréchal promised a regime stressing those values which had seemed lacking in pre-war France: order, discipline and unquestioning respect for church and state, but both Georges and Pauline had grave doubts that the elderly figurehead could make his resolutions stick with subordinates who consisted largely of fascists and collaborators.

In spite of the Vaniers' misgivings, the British and Canadian governments sought ways to support Pétain in the hope that Vichy would pursue a course independent of Germany. Moreover, in Canada, conservative Quebeckers viewed Pétain as the saviour of France, and applauded his promise to restore the traditional French values that up to the French Revolution of 1789 had linked the motherland so closely with Quebec.

The Vaniers argued the opposite view. They saw the politicians around Pétain as self-serving and unscrupulous, who, far from representing the real France, would not hesitate to sell it out to the Germans. The Vaniers kept insisting to the British and Canadian governments that only French Resistance leader Charles de Gaulle should be given the Allies' trust and support. "To us, there was clearly only one hope and that was de Gaulle," said Pauline.

De Gaulle had already established a reputation as a perceptive army strategist and was serving as Undersecretary for War when the Germans invaded France. But when Pétain made clear his plans to seek an armistice, de Gaulle strongly opposed the move and fled at once to England. There, he declared himself leader of the continuing French resistance and, in an emotional broadcast to France, he called on all Frenchmen to rally to his side. "France has lost a battle, but has not lost the war," he declared. "Let us fight to save her."

Both Vaniers remained convinced of the rightness of de Gaulle's cause and continued working tirelessly to encourage support for him. On many occasions, Pauline even dusted off her small portable typewriter to help out.

"From that point on, I was Georges' secretary during most of the war and there were times when I nearly went crazy. On one memorable night later in the war, we received a message from the Prime Minister at 2:00 in the morning asking Georges not only to prepare a speech for the people of France, but also to get the British Broadcasting Corporation to broadcast it before dawn. We searched the house for a room warm enough to work in and the best we could find was the bathroom. The only place I could sit was on the toilet. So there I was, my typewriter perched on my knees and Georges dictating the most lofty and emotional speech to France. I had the hardest time keeping a straight face as he was saying, '*La France ... L'honneur, la fierté, la gloire*' and there was I, typing on the toilet!"

Both Vaniers also turned their energies to helping the large numbers of refugees escaping to England. One of their first concerns was their faithful chauffeur, Joseph, who had insisted on returning to occupied Paris to search for his wife. Georges had given him the title to their personal car, which the Vaniers had been obliged to leave behind, but it served him little. Georges and Pauline managed to smuggle a letter to Joseph's wife, and in reply learned that Joseph had been caught by the Germans and sent to his death in the gas chambers. His sole crime was that of being a Jew.

Pauline wasted no time in linking up with the French Red Cross in London, and almost immediately began visiting hospitals in the southeast of England to check on the identity and welfare of French servicemen and refugees. "I set out every day in an army car — a mechanized transport car — to every hospital to find out where all the French wounded were. I found I could be particularly helpful to those who spoke no English, since only rarely did the hospital staff speak French.

"Each of the refugees had personal needs. They often wanted help contacting friends or relatives, or to be put in touch with agencies which could assist them.

"There were, alas, some I could not help, those who were too demoralized even to go on living. I remember one devastated young lad in the Rivers Green Hospital in Kent. He was in a ward of 48 French soldiers, all amputees. This poor boy was not mortally wounded, but one of his legs had been amputated and the injuries to the other did not appear to be healing. The nurses warned me that he seemed to be losing the will to live so I spent many long hours trying to help revive his interest in life and give him some hope.

"I told him he'd see France again and he showed me a photo of a young woman holding a baby. 'My wife,' he said simply, 'and she is expecting another child in a few months. Our town was almost entirely destroyed, and she has probably been killed. So why should I go on living?' I talked to him for a long time and, when I left, I said I'd be back the next morning. When I arrived, I found he had died in the night.

"The atmosphere of that ward was extraordinary. There was a man named Robert, a barber by trade, and, though he had been seriously wounded, he insisted on singing for his comrades the most beautiful arias from the *Barber of Seville* in his rich, baritone voice. He recovered from his wounds and we continued to correspond for several years afterwards.

"In all, they were a remarkable lot. They had been manning the forts of Dunkirk and were therefore on the last ship leaving for England. Their ship hit a mine and most of them were killed. Of the 80 men who were saved, 48 suffered amputations."

Linguistic difficulties, however, often prompted additional tragedies. Once in London's Hammersmith Hospital, officials told a ward of French servicemen they'd all be moved to Liverpool to avoid the bombing in London. The patients raised an uproar, made worse by their frustration at not being able to make any of the hospital staff understand them. Pauline recounts the incident:

"The hospital authorities were convinced they were facing a mutiny and were about to ask the police to remove them to prison facilities reserved for enemy aliens when I arrived on the scene. It seemed that the Frenchmen feared that a move to Liverpool was a step toward sending them back to France. They had all decided that, as soon as they were fit, they would join de Gaulle's Free French forces. They feared that if they were moved to Liverpool, they would miss the chance. So I called Malcolm Macdonald, then Minister of Health, and explained the story to him. He let them stay."

Another time, Pauline learned that the young son of a distinguished French admiral known to be sympathetic to de Gaulle, was being detained in a prison outside London. With great difficulty, she obtained permission to visit the lad.

"Off I went in a car driven by an army girl. When I arrived, there was barbed wire all around and we were stopped every few yards by sentries. As I got out of the car, a huge mob lunged towards me, speaking every sort of language — English, French, Polish and others. I managed to push through them and into the building where a tall man in civilian clothes showed me into an office. He sat opposite me, with two men on either side of him and I was put through the third degree. It was very frightening.

"When I was finally allowed to talk to the lad, I learned his story: the Germans were approaching the town in northern France where he was at school, and he feared they might hold him hostage in an attempt to force the collaboration of his father, a senior French naval technician. So he hitchhiked to the coast and found a ship whose crew said that, in exchange for all his money, they would take him to the southern French port where his father was based. Instead, however, the vessel went to England where he was abandoned. He felt betrayed and told British authorities he did not want to remain in England.

"The British concluded he must be a German collaborator and he was thrown with other suspect French refugees into this heavily guarded prison. The bewildered lad was barely 17. It took all the strings I could pull to get him released."

But of all Pauline's wartime experiences, the one involving her cousin, Philippe de Hauteclocque, touched her the deepest. Philippe was a French army colonel and known to the Germans as one of France's most brilliant military strategists. His unit had been surrounded in the early days of the war, and he had been captured, having received a serious head wound. He was an outspoken anti-Nazi, and Pauline feared for his life. Weeks passed without any news of his fate.

"One night, when I returned from my hospital rounds, Georges passed me the telephone with the remark, 'Here's someone who claims he knows you.' A familiar but unplaceable voice said to me, '*Bonjour, Pauline, this is François Leclerc.*' 'I'm sorry,' I answered, 'but I don't know anyone by that name.' 'Perhaps you know me better as Philippe,' he laughed. I screamed with delight and relief. He was at the railway station, and joined us at once, arriving with a bandaged head but buoyant spirits.

"That night, he recounted his tale. He explained that after his capture the Germans, having taken over the town of Lille, threw him into the city jail. He managed to pick the lock of his cell and slip past the dozing guards.

"He had to avoid the heavily protected bridge. Finding a dark spot along the river, he removed his clothes, wrapped them in his raincoat, and swam across. He then made his way south, hiding in ditches by day and walking by night. By the time he was caught again near Avalon, he was semi-conscious from hunger. The Germans put him under heavy guard on the third floor of a makeshift hospital. A nun serving as a nurse helped him escape by tying several sheets together and he lowered himself from the third floor window.

"He made his way to a country home owned by his sister. Thinking it was deserted, he broke in, only to find German troops waiting for him. Fortunately, however, one of the soldiers was a conscript from Czechoslovakia and had little use for the German cause. The soldier hid Philippe in the attic and smuggled food to him until he had regained enough strength to continue his flight.

"Friends Philippe met along the way urged him to assume an alias, change into farm clothes, burn his uniform and identity card, and accept a bicycle to speed him on his way to Bordeaux, where he had learned his wife was hiding.

"Along the way to Bordeaux, Philippe was welcomed by a country peasant, and together they listened to de Gaulle's stirring broadcast from London urging French servicemen to join the Free French forces. When Philippe finally located his family near Bordeaux, he assumed his wife would be opposed to any suggestion that he leave France to carry on the struggle. But, equally moved by de Gaulle's words, she said simply, 'How soon must you go?' He told me that if she hadn't said that, he wondered if he would have had the courage to leave. As it turned out, he left the next morning.

"Realizing that the Germans already suspected Philippe might be in Bordeaux, his friends in the newly forming French Resistance provided him with a false passport along with a Spanish visa in the name of François Leclerc. They also forged travel tickets from Lisbon to South America. Though he was arrested and briefly detained in Spain, he once again escaped, reached Lisbon and subsequently boarded a ship for England.

"In London, Philippe decided to keep the name Leclerc, even after he joined de Gaulle. He always feared for his family's safety if the Germans realized how Philippe de Hauteclocque had outwitted them. The night after he arrived, he broadcast a message to France that was really meant for his wife. My, it was moving! Some years after the war, he had become Maréchal Leclerc. Aside from de Gaulle, he probably contributed more than any other Frenchman to the German defeat, yet the Germans never realized who he was."

As evidence mounted of growing Vichy French collaboration with the Germans, the British became convinced that the French navy would fall into enemy hands. They therefore dispatched a naval task force to North Africa. When the captains of French warships there refused an ultimatum to join or surrender to the Allies, the French vessels were attacked and in most cases destroyed, with great loss of life among the crews. "You can imagine how warmly I was received after that by French servicemen in British hospitals," Pauline commented.

The Battle of Britain, fought in the air over England, began in earnest in the summer of 1940, with heavy German bombing raids occurring almost every night. "I can still remember our first night in a London 'shelter.' It was no more than a stuffy basement room, and a hit on the building above would have squashed us all like flies. Halfway through the bombardment the door flew open and a distressed man with a head shaped like an egg and a funny beaky nose burst in, dragging a pretty but equally distraught woman. Flustered and short of breath, he nonetheless managed to click his heels together and bow to us stiffly, announcing to our astonishment that he was in fact the Foreign Minister of Belgium. He and his companion had just escaped from his homeland and we spent the first night of the bombing together.

"Georges was so wonderful that night: he recounted a long string of humourous stories to keep up our morale, while bombs roared above and buildings collapsed around us."

Although Georges met frequently with de Gaulle, Pauline did only rarely. "He never had much time for women, but I do remember one difficult occasion when he said, 'Madame, I hear you are working with the Red Cross and with wounded French servicemen,' and he thanked me. Then he said, 'It is of course your duty to urge them as strongly as you can, threaten them if need be, to join with me as soon as they are able.'

"I knew I would lose the servicemen's confidence if I were as blatant as de Gaulle requested, and I would probably also forfeit British permission to make any hospital visits at all. So I tried to be as diplomatic as possible. 'General,' I said, 'of course I will inform them of your campaign, but neither the servicemen nor the British would welcome me applying the pressures you suggest. After all, my husband is a diplomat, and still accredited to Vichy France, so the only recommendations we can make publicly are those of our own government.'

"De Gaulle rose to his full 6 feet 5 inches, gave me a look of such disdain and said: 'And I thought you loved France!' It was lucky he was already stalking out of the room, for it was not easy for me to hold my tongue."

Meanwhile, the Germans were convinced they could destroy London, and with it the British will to resist. In spite of the unremitting aerial bombing, the Vaniers hung on through the worst of the blitz. "I could tell endless stories of the courage and resilience of the British in the face of this merciless onslaught. What impressed me the most was British unity in adversity: I never saw a single act of cowardice or defeatism.

"I once asked Georges if he felt it were safe for me to attend a high Mass on a Sunday afternoon. He reluctantly agreed, for most of the bombing was by night, but made me promise that if there were an air raid alert during the service, I would seek shelter.

"The church was packed, and the service had barely begun before an alert sounded. The priest turned round and said that anyone who wished to leave was welcome to do so, and could consider that they had in fact attended the entire Mass. Not one person left! It was then that I did the only heroic thing I did throughout the whole war: I waited until the Mass was resumed and, as I had promised Georges I would, I rose quietly and left the church.

"When I compare myself to the sang-froid of the English, I realize how childish some of my fears were. I have to confess that for the entire summer I took my bath at four in the afternoon, when bombings were rare, instead of at night. The reason I did was simple: I once heard that a woman had been having a bath when a bomb hit her house, and she was thrown out into the street stark naked. I felt I could survive a direct bomb hit, but I was not keen to be catapulted outside in the starkers!"

Pauline admitted she once did something some people called brave, even if Georges called it simply foolhardy. "There was a heavy daytime raid — it was the time the Germans hit Buckingham Palace — and we were deep in the shelter listening to the radio account of the ensuing dogfights. Suddenly it was announced that a Canadian fighter squadron had just arrived and was seeing its first combat action over London. So I climbed up to street level before anyone could stop me, and rushed out on the square to blow kisses to the pilots overhead. Georges later asked me how many engines the planes had, and I said proudly, 'At least two each!' He then told me I had been blowing kisses at the German bombers. Well, at least they had the courtesy not to drop one on me!"

Ottawa still persisted in its wishful thinking about Vichy. In December, without informing Georges, the Canadian government sent Pierre Dupuy, nominally Georges' junior officer as first secretary in the legation to France, on a visit to Vichy. Dupuy returned with glowing praise for the professed virtues of the Vichy regime, and made strong recommendations that Canada open full diplomatic relations with it. An exasperated Georges Vanier wrote directly to Prime Minister Mackenzie King asking that he be allowed to resign as Canadian Minister to France, if that meant Minister to the Vichy government. The letter was never formally acknowledged.

By the summer of 1940, however, the government began to agree with Georges that encouraging an independent stand by the Vichy government was futile. But Canada was not yet ready to give unqualified support to de Gaulle. Georges' continued presence in London urging the latter course was therefore proving an embarrassment. Thus, in August 1940, the decision was made to have the Vaniers return to Ottawa.

"We set off to leave London on an ominous date, September 13. I arrived at the station first, but a raid broke out and all train departures were postponed. So I went back home to our flat. Georges arrived at the station soon after, but guessed what had happened and immediately returned to the flat as well, even though by then bombs were falling everywhere. We learned later that only seconds after his departure from the station, two bombs had fallen within twenty yards from the very spot where we had intended to meet each other.

"Sobered by this experience, we waited until the 'all clear' sounded, then, from another station boarded a train heading north to Glasgow. We had been through almost a year of non-stop bombing, and it was such a relief to be getting out of London. But I still felt ashamed. I felt I was running away like a coward.

"When we got to Glasgow, we found to our delight that our reservations were for a Canadian vessel, the venerable Canadian Pacific passenger ship, the *Empress of Australia*. There were many people we knew on board, and at least 300 children who were being evacuated."

While the ship sat for five days in the Firth of Clyde, the Vaniers watched in horror as bombs pounded the city of Glasgow; one bomb even exploded in the funnel of a nearby cruiser. On the BBC news, they heard that another ship, the *City of Benares,* which had just set sail ahead of them, had been torpedoed, resulting in enormous loss of life, particularly among the several hundred children on board.

The Vaniers' departure was delayed because the German battle cruiser *Scharnhorst* was wreaking havoc along the route their convoy had planned to take. "In spite of all these ominous signs, there was not a single complaint from anyone on board. In the end we set off in the dead of night in a convoy with four other ships. At dawn, I went up on deck and saw a Sunderland flying boat overhead and noticed there were two corvettes escorting us. So I felt more secure.

"To our surprise, however, we headed south, not west. Somewhere near the Azores, the hot and humid islands off the coast of Portugal, our ship signalled good-bye to the convoy and our escorts. It had been decided that with the *Empress's* speed we should best go it alone, and hope to outrun both German U-boats and the *Scharnhorst*. We were told not to undress for sleeping at night, but to remain in our weatherproof fatigues, with our lifebelts well strapped on.

"We were never to know the reasons for so many abrupt changes of course at all hours of day and night. But we had met the captain when we first came on board — a rosy-faced eager young man who seemed barely 30, and was bursting with energy. We did not see him again until the ship docked in Halifax where he was being helped ashore, a haggard, burnt-out shadow of a man who looked 70. He had not left his place on the bridge for 14 days.

"Yes, that was a trip I will never forget. I can tell you that after it was over, Canada never looked so good!"

9
Seeking Support in Canada (1940-1943)

The Vaniers' return to Canada turned out to be a bitter experience. Their finances allowed them to rent only a small basement apartment in Montreal. Georges was given no job until the following year, and then only a part-time post with the new U.S./Canada Joint Defence Board. The bitterest blow of all was that many of their old friends would have nothing to do with them because of their denunciation of the Vichy regime.

"Yes, our new life was difficult. Our support of de Gaulle was well known and, when we came to Quebec, there weren't many Gaullists there — there were some, but not many. On the first day I arrived I met an old friend whose wife was French. She turned out to be a Pétainist and, when she heard I supported de Gaulle, she didn't talk to me for the rest of our stay in Canada. Such incidents happened constantly. It was too painful.

"Then we went to Ottawa and stayed a fortnight with the Athlones (The Earl of Athlone, who was Governor General, and Princess Alice) at Government House. But it wasn't easy. Like many others, they weren't too sure of us and could not understand our determined stand for de Gaulle. So our visit was very strained, to say the least."

They were also struck by Canadians' indifference to the war. "We had been through so much, but when we returned home we realized that Canada had been so far removed from Europe that many Canadians could not grasp the seriousness of events over there — the cruelty and suffering of war, the German atrocities, the risks incurred by refugees, the nightly destruction of London. It all seemed far too remote to be believed.

"It was incredible to find people complaining of rations, complaining that they didn't have enough sugar. Georges was more controlled than I was. I would get so angry I'd slam doors and leave whenever anyone started talking that way.

"I could understand the anxiety and anguish of mothers whose sons were in the service, but I just couldn't understand anyone complaining about anything here in Canada. They just had no idea what real deprivation meant.

"We tried to speak about what we had seen in Europe and to bring home the threat a German victory would pose to Canada, but our words fell on deaf ears. Worse still, we often met with violent rejection. We were accused of being frauds and deliberate liars. I remember being invited to speak at a luncheon at the Mount Royal Hotel in Montreal, and I was introduced as 'the great pretender.' I was so hurt I could not open my mouth and had to walk out."

Georges met similar reactions. At one point he was apparently becoming such an embarrassment to the Canadian Government that he was offered an embassy post in Latin America just to remove him from the country. "Of course we turned it down. Our place was in Canada as long as we could do anything to bring home to our compatriots the need for our country to do its share in the war.

"But antipathy towards us was deeply entrenched: we started receiving threatening letters and phone calls. Meetings we addressed were broken up by or- ganized mobs; outrageous accusations were whispered and even printed in the press about us, our personal lives, even about our children.

"On top of all this, and to my astonishment at the age of 43, I found myself pregnant! This was considered, incredibly enough, a further lapse of conservative morality, or at least good taste, and several erstwhile friends reproached me bitterly — not for having a child at 43, but for still doing what's necessary to *have* a child at such an age!

"It proved a difficult pregnancy, but in the end it had a happy resolution: Michel Paul was born a healthy baby in July 1941 and we christened him in what was then St. James (now Mary Queen of the World) Cathedral on August 13. We felt certain that Michel would be a portent of better times to come. True enough, two days after his christening, the Prime Minister announced Georges' promotion to the rank of brigadier-general and his appointment to command the military district of Quebec."

Georges Vanier was back on the job. The family moved to Quebec in September and took over the District Commander's official residence on St-Louis Street.

There was hard work to be done. French-speaking Canadians were not convinced that a European war was relevant to far-off Canada and were not about to risk their lives for such a distant cause. Georges thus worked diligently to improve conditions in the armed forces for French-speaking Canadians and to attract more recruits. He also spent much of his time touring Quebec, stressing both the danger to Canada if the Germans were not stopped, and the need for French Canada to play its part in the country's defence.

Pauline was equally active. She crisscrossed the province, speaking in far-flung towns and villages. "I travelled across the whole of Quebec, right to the Gaspé. At every stop, I'd visit the *curé* and ask to speak in the parish hall. Then I'd talk about the dangers of war and the consequences of a German victory. And of course I'd urge wives and mothers to work for the war effort and to invest in government war bonds.

"People in those quiet and isolated villages along the lower St. Lawrence were impossible to convince. But that suddenly changed when the Germans made a serious tactical blunder. A German submarine landed a spy in the area, equipped with outdated Canadian money. A hotel owner spotted the error, quietly accepted his dollar bills, then telephoned the police; the man was arrested on a train to Montreal. That incident, along with the growing number of ships being sunk by U-boats in the Gulf of St. Lawrence, brought home to even the remotest Quebeckers the fact that Germany posed a threat to Canada just as much as it did to Europe."

An incident during one of Pauline's speaking tours of the Gaspé brought the tragedy of war even closer. She and Georges had earlier known a young French Canadian airman, Jacques Chevrier, "a very remarkable man and one we had come to know much like a son." He had taken part in the Battle of Britain and was now training other pilots in Canada. Passing the RCAF (Royal Canadian Air Force) station at Mont Joli where he was stationed, Pauline decided to call Jacques. "We spoke on the telephone and he said he would try to meet with me the next morning at Mass in the village church, and we could have breakfast afterwards.

"The next morning, I went early to Mass but he never arrived. I waited for him at breakfast and he still didn't turn up. Then, suddenly, I was overwhelmed with a sense of foreboding. I had to leave at 10:00 a.m. for a speaking engagement at Matane. When I arrived at my hotel, I met an airman and asked for news of Jacques Chevrier. He looked up at me and said simply that he had disappeared. I knew in my heart that something had happened to him. I stopped by the church to ask the *curé* to say a mass for him and the *curé* told me he had heard a plane in the early morning flying so low that he knew something must be wrong. Later in Matane two villagers told me that they had seen a plane fall into the sea a few miles from Cap Chat. I finally sought out the squadron's second-in-command and asked him what had happened. He told me that Jacques Chevrier was missing and must be presumed dead. There was never any wreckage of his aircraft found, nor was it ever established whether he was shot down or if he crashed. His disappearance remains a mystery to this day.

"Georges and I were stunned. He was such a remarkable young man, solidly French Canadian, and deeply religious. His disappearance in the St. Lawrence had something very symbolic about it. Georges wrote a beautiful epitaph for this boy, which gives you an idea how much he meant to us both:

"'*He was proud to wear over his heart the wings that he had carried in the Battle of Britain — the wings that one summer night were folded over the waters of the St. Lawrence. They were broken then, but God stepped down to pick them up.'*"

It was that same year that Jock, then barely 13, dropped a bombshell of his own on his parents. "Georges returned home one day and announced that he had received a strange note from Jock saying he wished to see his father at his office on a matter of great seriousness. It was obviously, in Jock's mind, a business matter between men so they arranged an appointment at Georges' office. There, Jock announced to his father that he had decided to join the navy, and that he planned to enter the Royal Naval College in England.

"Georges was bowled over. After all, Jock was only 13. But it was clear he was serious: he had already obtained the requisite application form and needed only his father's consent in writing to complete it, plus letters of recommendation and a certificate of good health.

"I opposed the idea desperately, but Georges was of two minds. 'Jock knows what war is all about,' he pointed out. 'He's lived through our escape from France and the air raids on London; when we stop a child who is determined to do something, and it turns out to have been a great opportunity missed, he may end up reproaching us for the rest of his life.'

"I must confess I was selfishly unfair with Jock. I took him for a walk and tried to scare him off the idea. 'Suppose you were injured or fell sick,' I asked him. 'There might be no way we could come to you, let alone help you out.' 'But Mummy,' I remember him saying, 'I just *have* to go!'

"He was a funny child at that age, rather small, terribly thin and scrawny. But the Admiralty accepted him, and told him to prepare himself to join the spring term of 1942.

"I worried so much as he readied to leave for England. I remember packing his steamer trunk, tears flooding the clothing as I stuffed chocolate and candy between the layers. Then Georges travelled with him by train to Halifax, saw him onto the ship and off he went, all by himself, to cross the Atlantic and embark on a naval career. All this at 13. That was one of the hardest things I ever did.

"Jock reached London safely, reported to the Admiralty and was sent off to the Naval College in Dartmouth. The only mishap was that his trunk, which contained his brand-new uniform, got lost en route and he had to survive the first days at College in gray shorts and a blazer while all his fellow students were properly attired in their new uniforms."

It would be almost a year before the Vaniers would see Jock again. "The Naval College was moved from Dartmouth to Eaton Hall in Cheshire so we had to travel to Cheshire to see him. When we arrived at the station, there stood a tall, thin asparagus in front of us.

The smallish five-footer who had left us at the age of 13 was now, one year later, over six feet tall!"

After Georges' mission to persuade French Canadians to join the war effort was essentially accomplished, he longed to return to the front lines in Europe. On November 11, 1942 — the date of the World War I armistice in 1918 — he wrote to External Affairs: "I hope it is not necessary to remind you that the former Minister to France hopes and prays that he will be allowed to continue the work begun in 1939." On November 30, the Prime Minister approved Georges' appointment as Minister to the Allied Governments in London (eight of the occupied European states but not France) with powers as well "to consult with the French National Committee" (de Gaulle and the Free French) on all matters of mutual interest relating to the conduct of the war." This reference, which did not recognize the Free French as a government in exile, was a discreet way of finally withdrawing Canadian recognition of the Vichy government.

Georges was delayed in taking up his new post by a serious bout of pneumonia. He was hospitalized for more than a month, often with temperatures soaring to 105 degrees. Consequently, he was not able to fly to England until March 1943.

Pauline found herself in a dilemma. "I was very perturbed about what and where my duty was. I had Byngsie, Bernard, and Michel, a tiny baby of 18 months whom I was loathe to leave in Canada, and yet I had Thérèse and Jock and my husband in England. Where should I go?"

She had also not been well herself and her doctor had recommended a major operation, while strongly advising her against any travelling. "I also guessed correctly, as things turned out, that Georges would follow de Gaulle into the fighting and liberation of France, and I wondered if I would not be more of a handicap than a help to him."

Pauline's devoted mother ("Ganna" to the children) was ready to step in again and offer her invaluable help. In spite of her age and fragility, she offered to take care of the youngest children, even baby Michel, whom she especially adored.

"However, I was still uncertain whether I should join Georges and the two children in England or remain with the others in Canada. So I had a little talk with the Lord, and said, 'If it is my duty to follow Georges to London, please give me a sign.' Then something happened to me that is really uncanny. When I went back to see my doctor, he took a further X-ray and couldn't believe what it revealed; there was absolutely no trace of the ailment I'd had up till that time. It had completely disappeared. So I took that as a sign that the Lord wanted me to go — that and the fact that my mother was able to look after the children. I still don't know if I was entirely right, but in wartime you do things that aren't always wise. So I made ready to take the first available means of transport to London."

The "first available means" turned out to be yet another adventure for Pauline Vanier. "External Affairs arranged for me to travel to Baltimore, Maryland, by train. Three nights later, I was picked up by bus late at night and driven to a nearby naval base. There I boarded a lumbering flying boat which took off in complete darkness on the first leg of our flight to England. The seats were simple, fabric bucket seats, except for one bunk, which was occupied by a distinguished fellow passenger, Lord Beaverbrook, the Canadian newspaper magnate and wartime British government minister.

"It was the first time I had ever flown and I was terrified. The aircraft landed somewhere in Newfoundland in the early dawn, and we were all taken to Quonset huts to spend the day. At 7:00 p.m., the plane took off again, and when dawn broke next morning we found ourselves being escorted by two Spitfire fighter planes over Ireland. We landed near Shannon, on the west coast of Ireland, and some boisterous Irish army recruits took us to a pub for a rollicking breakfast of bacon and eggs."

The aircraft flew on unescorted to Poole, near Bournemouth, England, where a relieved Georges Vanier greeted his wife. He reported that German fighter aircraft had been over Poole less than an hour before, and the cumbersome flying boat would have been easy prey.

Georges and Pauline travelled by train to London and settled into a small flat near Piccadilly. "I could hardly believe I was back here starting a new life once again," Pauline sighed.

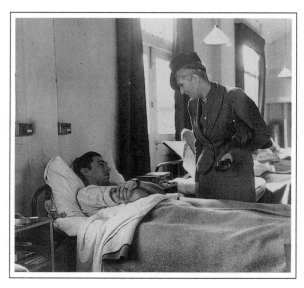

Pauline Vanier chatting with a wounded soldier at No. 17 Canadian General Hospital, Pine Wood, England, 1943.

(Canadian Military HQ PR Branch/DND/National Archives of Canada PA 166099.)

Villa Simian, the Vanier's luxurious home outside Algiers.

(National Archives of Canada, PA 185486.)

10
London and Algiers
(1943-1944)

Georges set up his legation in a modest office near Berkeley Street. As Canadian Minister to the Allied Governments in Exile, he was kept at arm's length from the Canadian High Commission but was nevertheless in close touch with their diplomats accredited to Britain.

"It was a curious, almost unreal life we led," said Pauline. "There was much socializing with old guard politicians from the occupied European countries — such a conglomeration of nations! Many of the politicians seemed quite detached from the realities of their own homelands, but all too aware that resistance forces in those lands might have little use for them when their countries were finally liberated. As a result, we often felt we were somehow on the periphery of events, doing nothing that was very useful."

By this time, their children were also getting involved in the war effort. Thérèse had joined the British Army Mechanized Transport Corps and worked at the Free French officers training school as secretary and driver to the commandant. Later she transferred to the Canadian Women's Army Corps, unflatteringly referred to as the "Quacks."

"Thérèse graduated first in her officers' training class at Wellington Barracks, which prompted Georges to say she had learned a most unfeminine number of ways in which even the strongest of men could be permanently disabled!"

One of Thérèse's colleagues in the Free French was a handsome young man named Leopold who was obviously very much in love with her. "I remember he came with Thérèse to dinner late in the autumn, and, as he left, he said, 'Madame, would you be kind enough to pray for me around Christmastime?' I promised I would, but did not of course ask him what he would be doing at that time.

"Shortly after Christmas, I was alone in our flat. Georges had left for a visit to Algiers, newly taken by the Americans from the Vichy forces. The doorbell rang, and there was a figure in a ragged commando camouflage outfit, face blackened. I didn't recognize him, and his appearance was frightening. It wasn't until he took off his helmet that I saw it was Leopold.

"He could hardly walk from fatigue, but asked only if he could come in and rest. I insisted he take a stiff drink and some nourishment, and at least allow time for a bath and a sleep while I repaired his clothes. But he was gone all too soon; I did not ask him what he had been involved in, and he did not volunteer to say. Within a month, however, his name appeared prominently in the latest list of decorations won by Allied servicemen. The citation gave few details, saying only that in the face of intense enemy fire and at great risk to his own life, he had saved the life of his commanding officer."

On December 30, 1943, Georges Vanier climbed aboard an ancient RAF (Royal Air Force) aircraft and flew to Algiers. When General de Gaulle moved his headquarters there, so did Georges Vanier, anxious to provide evidence of what was now Canada's unqualified support for the General's leadership.

This was a period of anxiety for Pauline, who stayed in London. "I was going through quite a spiritual experience at the time and that took more out of me than any war matters. After George left, I felt terribly alone in the flat in Arlington House. The bombing continued spasmodically and there were times when I was very frightened. Those were difficult weeks and I felt a very deep need to hang onto my spiritual life. So nearly every day, I climbed on a bus and travelled up to Ladbroke Grove to visit the Carmelites. I would never have gotten through those tumultuous times without the help of those sisters."

Pauline was also tiring of her superficial social life among the expatriot European diplomats, and yearned to join Georges on the front lines in North Africa. At length, Christopher Eberts, Georges' second-in-command at the legation in London, found a way.

"The British were flying out a newly appointed air attaché to Algiers, and there was a spare seat in the old twin-engined Dakota aircraft that would be making the trip. So the air attaché and I took the train to Bristol, got out of the train and were appalled to discover that the city had just been flattened by bombing. We then got in a bus and went to a nearby airport.

"We took another flight leaving at midnight and it was all very hush-hush. I sat next to a girl and in the dark noticed she had a rosary tangled up in her hand. And so did I!

"As soon as the plane left Bristol, the pilot ordered us to tie on our Mae West life jackets, an ominous omen! Without insulation, the Dakota was anything but comfortable. The cabin temperature dropped to near zero, we were in complete darkness and the noise of the engines made any conversation impossible!

"While it was still dark, the aircraft started losing altitude and seemed to be circling aimlessly. We peered out the windows, wondering if we were coming down at sea, when suddenly, the Rock of Gibraltar burst into light directly below us, lit by what seemed to be a hundred searchlights. Apparently airport authorities heard our plane and feared we were about to crash into it!

"We landed safely on the tiny airstrip at the north end of the Rock, and found rest and warmth in a nearby hotel. When we returned to the frigid Dakota that evening, we learned that General Sikorski, the Polish Premier-in-exile, had been killed in a plane crash taking off from the same airstrip a short time before. This didn't make the atmosphere too cheerful!

"We flew again through the night and when dawn broke, the pilot invited me into the cockpit as we passed along the North African coast. I sat in the seat behind him and he banked the plane at the most terrifying angle, explaining that it was just a signal to show who we were! Along the coast, the water was clear as glass and we passed several convoys. It was a most extraordinary flight.

"All in all, it took two full days to reach Algiers. No one was expecting me since wives are virtually never allowed to join their husbands on missions in wartime. I think also the legation in London may have been reluctant to tell Georges I was coming in case I never got there!"

Pauline finally linked up with a delighted Georges who drove her to their new home: a luxurious colonial mansion named Villa Simian. The mansion had been requisitioned for Georges and his small team at Chéragas, some 25 kilometres west of Algiers. Pauline was stunned by its opulence. "When I walked in the door, the first thing I saw were baskets and baskets of oranges and lemons. I hadn't seen such fruit in England since the war began!" A staff of five Algerian servants was on hand, and, judging from the resonant Arabic singing that kept Pauline awake much of the night, dozens of their families also lived on the estate. "It was the Moslem sacred month of Ramadan so they started their festive parties after sunset. The din was unbelievable!"

Georges' mission in Algiers was to liaise with de Gaulle, his Free French forces and the French politicians-in-exile waiting to take over a soon-to-be liberated France. But for Pauline, the extravagance of the villa lifestyle in the midst of a war that was practically reducing Europe to starvation seemed totally wrong. Equally wrong, from Pauline's viewpoint, were the self-promoting French officials who laughed in derision at her enquiries as to whether the Algerians themselves were being consulted about the conduct of the war or the future of their homeland.

"The French politicians spent most of their time bad-mouthing each other and jostling for power among themselves. As they boasted about how they would impose their will on France after they had 'liberated' it, their loose talk was actually betraying the soldiers and servicemen, both French and Allied, who were doing the real liberating. These gallant young men were parachuting into France, Italy, Greece and Yugoslavia at enormous risk to support resistance fighters. Far too many of them were leaving Algiers on missions behind enemy lines and never coming back.

"I remember one time a British submarine captain taking me aside and asking me if there were anything I could do to seal the lips of his French liaison officer. This officer was telling everyone how he had arranged for the submarine captain to initiate regular trips to supply resistance workers at a secret cove in southern France. He then would give its location to anyone who asked!

"It is impossible to describe the atmosphere in Algiers during that period : a mixture of heroism and decadence that would make the film *Casablanca* seem a masterpiece of understatement.

"I remember one famous occasion when Diana Cooper, the wife of the British ambassador Duff Cooper, decided to do her bit for the international resistance fighters who were waiting in Algiers to be dropped behind enemy lines. So she threw the most extraordinary party — Diana really has a sense of the dramatic — and she invited dozens of the very smart, beautiful and unattached French society women in Algiers. There was a full moon, the champagne was flowing and there was much merriment.

"Among the guests were 20 Yugoslav freedom fighters slated to be flown out on a parachute drop the next night. The chic and sophisticated French ladies, however, wanted nothing to do with the down-to-earth Yugoslavs, but the Yugoslavs took the slight in good spirit: they said they would offer their own entertainment for the party. So they sang as a choir in such perfect harmony the passionate, heart-rending songs of freedom of their homeland. Their voices were rich and resonant Slav voices. We didn't need to know the words: they were obviously singing of life and death, of suffering and exile and, someday, God willing, of triumph. I found it all quite overwhelming as they sang their hearts out, and wrenched my own.

"Suddenly, the smart society ladies and their French politician companions, having grown tired of listening, abruptly began gossipping in deliberately sharp and loud voices. It was all too obvious what they meant: we don't want to hear any more of your music. You may indeed be going off to die for our nation's liberty, but we're not interested in your hopes and dreams!

"Something inside me snapped. I leapt to my feet and cried out to the group of ladies, 'That's enough! I can't stand any more of your chattering. Can't you show some respect?' I wanted to say much more to them, but a shocked silence descended and I realized I would create a scandal if I continued. So I walked out, followed by a dozen other guests. But even before we got through the doors the din of those women had resumed at full volume."

Pauline and Georges were to spend almost six months in Algiers and North Africa. The decadence notwithstanding, it was an exhilarating, heady period and they welcomed a succession of important visitors to their home. Charles de Gaulle and his wife dined with them frequently ("We'd go to them or they'd come to us"); Glubb Pasha, the British soldier who commanded the Arab Legion, visited ("He actually came as 'Mr. Smith' and we didn't know who he was until after he left!"). Harold MacMillan, later British Prime Minister, and the French social activist, Abbé Pierre, also visited. In addition, countless members of the Resistance found their way to the Vanier home for rest, fellowship and encouragement. In fact, Resistance heroine Elizabeth de Miribel, a frequent visitor who became a life-long friend of the Vaniers, christened their home "the house of the Resistance."

One of their most emotional visits during this period was by Pauline's cousin, Philippe de Hauteclocque, who, still under the pseudonym Leclerc, had liberated the vast French colonial holdings in Equatorial and West Africa from Vichy control with a relative handful of Free French fighters. His division was among the Allied forces liberating France, and it was to Leclerc that the German garrison in Paris surrendered on August 26.

Pauline Vanier also welcomed to her home dozens of young Canadians from a nearby parachute training camp, who found with the Vaniers a second home while they were waiting to be parachuted into occupied territories. "I was able to write to their families to tell them they were well and were leaving on special missions. I also told them not to worry if they didn't receive word for several weeks. I did this for every single Canadian. Some of them kept in touch with me for years afterwards. But there were always others whom I never heard from again, and I'd lie in bed at night wondering if they ever survived their mission."

Pauline spoke often about those intense days and how, spiritually, she felt more fully alive at that time than ever before. She felt very close to God as she consoled and encouraged those courageous young fighters and supported them in her prayers.

"Nobody can possibly imagine what it was like in Algiers at that time. I don't think I've ever lived so intensely as I lived during those months."

With the Allied landings in Normandy in June 1944, Georges began pressing Ottawa to arrange for his return to London, so he could be among the first of the Allied forces to enter a liberated Paris. But Paris surrendered to Leclerc on August 26, and it was not until September that Ottawa agreed that Georges could leave Algiers. They then proposed simply to transport him to London by sea, a perilous three-week undertaking. Happily, Ambassador Cooper found both Vaniers a lift by air; they left together in a British bomber and arrived back in London September 4. Despite warnings that Paris was still filled with German and collaborationist snipers, Georges was determined to be the first ambassador accredited to France to return to the French capital. Pauline was equally determined to accompany him. After all, she had a bet with her daughter Thérèse as to who would be the first to reach the reilluminated "City of Light."

11
Return to Liberated France
(1944-1953)

As Georges Vanier waited impatiently in London for his opportunity to return to Paris, Pauline Vanier learned that the Allied Command had decreed it unsafe for a wife to enter Paris, at least for the foreseeable future — there was serious food rationing and sporadic sniping. The conspiring Pauline, however, learned that if she had an official position, preferably one with a uniform, she might obtain permission. She first turned to the Canadian Women's Army Corps but they told her bluntly that to impersonate a member of the Corps would be a serious military offence.

Undeterred, she decided to appoint herself a representative of the Canadian Red Cross. Although the Red Cross agreed, finding a uniform was no easy task. Only one member of the Canadian Red Cross in Britain had a uniform that would fit the tall, full figure of Pauline Vanier, and that member was away on leave and there was no time to have one made. Pauline found the perfect solution: she would "borrow" the uniform from the absentee owner, while she commissioned a new one to be ready for the owner's return.

"To say it fitted was an exaggeration. I could barely squeeze the skirt over my hips, the sleeves hardly

Laying a wreath on the grave of the unknown soldier at the Canadian cemetary, Dieppe, France, 1944.

(Frank Duberville/DND/Public Archives of Canada, PA 141882.)

The Vaniers welcoming Prime Minister Mackenzie King to the Paris Peace Conference, 1946.

(Agence Photographique Keystone/National Archives of Canada, PA 16472.)

covered my elbows and the jacket was too short. I couldn't find anyone to alter it, so I did the best I could myself. And the hat flapped about and made me look like a dying duck. Oh my! I must have looked like nothing on earth. But it was enough to get me on the plane to Paris with Georges."

They arrived in Paris just 12 days after its liberation — Georges Vanier as Canada's newly appointed Ambassador and, much to his delight, the first ambassador to enter liberated France. To celebrate their safe landing, he had reserved rooms at his favourite hotel, the Ritz, and he invited the whole crew to a celebratory champagne lunch at the hotel.

Dining in the hotel that evening, the Vaniers gave the waiter their order for food, but said they would forgo drinks. The waiter then disappeared. After more than an hour's wait, they asked when they would be served. "Oh," said the waiter disdainfully, "the manager says that anyone who does not order wine with his meal is not to be served anything!" Apparently even the most junior German officers of the occupation ordered drinks with their dinner at the Ritz, and "Canadians should know better than to do anything less." The Vaniers changed hotels the next morning.

That next day, while in their new hotel room, there was a knock on the door and in walked a tall figure in combat gear, long rubber boots and a heavy steel helmet. "My first reaction was 'What an extraordinary apparition!' The figure removed its helmet and I realized that it was Thérèse! She had just arrived by jeep. She had lost her bet on being the first Vanier into Paris, but not by much."

While Georges became fully engrossed in monitoring, and often influencing, the restoration of democratic government in liberated France, Pauline wasted no time in fulfilling her role as Canadian Red Cross representative. She speedily organized two clubs for

Canadian servicemen, and recruited volunteer hostesses to operate them and organize dances and visits to the theatre and cultural events.

"By November we were welcoming more than 400 guests daily. When we were short-handed, I would help out in the kitchen. As ambassadors from other countries began arriving in Paris, their wives were often aghast at the sight of this woman in the ill-fitting uniform and floppy felt hat dishing out soup. Someone told me later that the Canadian Red Cross had no right to allow me to act as their agent in France. Actually, as the wife of an ambassador, I probably should not have done what I did. But I could never face myself if I were in France at that time and not doing something to help."

For their first six months in Paris, the Vaniers lived in an apartment-hotel that had been occupied by the Germans. "It was such a dingy place; we were virtually surrounded by packing cases and dust. When the war in Europe ended in May, we decided it was time to start being civilized so we began looking for a better apartment, specially one that would be suitable for diplomatic entertaining.

"The first place we were shown was a large mansion on the elegant Boulevard Haussmann. We were taken there by an agent and ushered in by a thin, macabre man dressed entirely in black. The first things we noticed were German officers' tunics hanging in the hall; in the dining room we found half-full bottles of champagne, glasses knocked over and fragments of rotting food uneaten. Obviously, the previous inhabitants had left in one great hurry. We quickly decided against that one.

"Another place we were offered was an extraordinary apartment on the Left Bank, furnished in opulent 1920s style, with black lacquered furniture, mauve carpets, little cubic tables that looked like coffins for babies, and ostrich feather quilts everywhere. There was also a cupboard full of dresses and hats and mink coats. We learned that it had belonged to a

112

Frenchwoman who'd been a mistress of a senior Gestapo officer. They'd both been caught in the act and were now in prison. We decided to let that one pass too."

They eventually found an apartment at the Vendôme on the rue Castiglione. They settled in and Pauline returned to her self-appointed duties. "Refugees of all nations, specially from Poland, were flooding into Paris, often friendless and destitute. So we managed to obtain and distribute a huge shipment of clothing for Polish refugees, many of them homeless after the Russian annexation of the eastern half of Poland."

Encouraged by her success in obtaining emergency provisions for the Poles, Pauline urged the Red Cross to send more and larger shipments which she could distribute to others in need, among them destitute French who were prevented by red tape from getting help from French agencies. "Help came from everywhere and we were able to dispense more than a million dollars' worth of food, clothing and essential supplies, including over 5000 layettes (kits for newborn babies).

"When I realized there was no more milk in Paris, I sent a message to London and within a week two Dakotas brought over several tons of milk powder, butter and jam. Imagine my feeling of joy when I could distribute all that! This was so wonderful for me, the giving. I'm not as good at receiving but I've always been able to give."

With their relief operation quickly becoming too large for its quarters in the legation, the Canadian Royal Bank stepped in and supplied badly needed staff and offices. "My secretary and right hand was Christine Boulache, someone I had rescued from virtual destitution and whose story is all too typical of the times. She had joined the Resistance in 1943, and, to avoid endangering her family, had left home and worked far from her village. Her concern not to expose her family was in vain, however. Although the

Germans did not catch her, they did learn where she had come from, arrested her elderly parents and two brothers, destroyed their home and deported them to Germany, where they all perished in concentration camps. At war's end, Christine was penniless, and was told she could not obtain help from French agencies because her story could not be verified.

The New Year (1945) brought Allied advances into Germany itself. In their wake, more and more concentration camps were liberated, and the trickle of refugees became a flood. Liberating forces were unable to cope with the swelling numbers, and camp inmates who were fit enough to travel — and often even those who were not — were simply given a railway ticket to Paris and told to fend for themselves. Aware of this practice, Pauline convinced other agencies to join with her in organizing reception services at the station.

"We greeted the refugees with drinks, refreshments, clothes and survival kits, and tried to reach their families, friends or anyone who might take them in. Many, however, had no idea whether anyone they knew was still alive, let alone their whereabouts. For them, we arranged temporary shelter. Then we took their photos and stuck these up on long panels lining both sides of the railway station in hopes that someone in the crowds would recognize the name or the picture of a long-lost relative or friend.

"It was obvious that what the refugees needed most was psychiatric care and counselling, even before physical rehabilitation. So we spoke at length to each new arrival, encouraging them to talk of their experiences, and persuading them that we could understand what they had been through.

"But many were too psychologically wounded to respond. I remember one desperate case, a withered shell of a man, whom I tried for an hour to reach. Finally, in resignation, I said, 'Well, no matter what you've been through, at least you've survived, and can begin a new life, here, where you're at home.' To my astonishment he finally spoke. 'Really?' he asked, and pulled back his sleeve to show the Star of David burnt into his flesh. 'Auschwitz,' he said simply. I pressed him to say more and he told me that he and his Jewish family had been betrayed by their neighbours in Paris in exchange for a five-franc reward from the German Gestapo. He had been taken to Auschwitz where his parents, his wife, and their children had been thrown into the gas chamber in front of his eyes. 'Home?' he asked finally. 'Where is my home?'

"I tried to arrange psychiatric counselling for him but he refused to accept my efforts; I tried to keep in touch with him and others among the most distressing cases we met, but all too often their stories ended the same way: in lonely suicides, or death from the physical privations they had suffered."

Certainly, it was the Jewish people in France who suffered the most during the war. One of Pauline's co-workers, a Catholic woman, early in the occupation stumbled upon a Gestapo round-up of Jews. The Gestapo had forced one hundred adults into a single cattle truck for deportation to Germany. To further demoralize the captives, the Germans had separated them from their children.

"The courageous woman succeeded in rounding up about 25 of the Jewish youngsters, and led them off to her house in Paris where they hid for the night. Realizing the children would soon be caught there, she managed to smuggle them across the border into unoccupied Vichy France, and took them by night to a house in the hills owned by relatives.

"She tried to keep their presence secret from the local villagers, but every day she had to come into the village to buy provisions. One day she returned home to find to her horror that the children had been locked in the house and the house burnt to the ground, every child dead and their bodies barely identifiable. Pro-

Pétainist members of the village had apparently decided they would go one better than their friends the Germans when it came to Jews."

Children were often the greatest losers during the war. Even after liberation, large gangs of orphaned or abandoned children roamed the streets of Paris, living on garbage and the proceeds of theft and petty crime. Sensitive to these developments, Pauline helped a French priest-worker organize a home in the countryside for 50 of these youngsters. She also persuaded the Canadian Massey-Harris company to donate a tractor to help the institution operate a farm and become self-supporting.

In addition, Pauline threw herself behind the work of Abbé Pierre who set up housing and workshops for the homeless of Paris. Many wartime privations had left these people too physically sapped to hold down a job, and they were thus dying in the cold winters of post-war France. For them and for hundreds of others living on abandoned barges in the Seine, Pauline journeyed to Toronto to accept thousands of dollars worth of supplies donated by the T. Eaton company.

Pauline was also able to intercede with military authorities to help find people who had been imprisoned in German concentration camps and she met dozens of people, who had themselves survived the horrors of the camps, as they arrived in Paris. "For weeks, we did nothing else but meet people who'd been in concentration camps. We even had a dinner party for some of them organized with Elizabeth de Miribel. We invited President de Gaulle's young niece who had just been released from two years in Ravensbruck, another young girl of 19 who had been in solitary confinement for two years and five or six of the most extraordinary Resistance people just released from camps. We got so involved with these people who'd been through such dreadful experiences. You can imagine the intensity of our lives during those heart-wrenching days."

The liberation of France provided an opportunity for the settling of many wartime debts and injustices. Many of the most vengeful Resistance workers were relatively new participants in the movement, the "last-minute" Resisters of 1945. To cover what often amounted to their own collaboration with the enemy, they were quick to accuse of treason any who might expose them.

Many Frenchmen sought to escape retribution by fleeing to Canada, one country that had established a reputation of openness to refugees from persecution. When such persons approached the Canadian Embassy, it was to Pauline Vanier that they turned.

"Dozens of people came to see me, perhaps because by then I had gained a certain reputation for discretion and sympathy, or perhaps simply because I was a woman, a wife and a mother. In any case, they seemed to prefer coming to me rather than to an embassy official. My problem was determining which ones were innocent and were fleeing unjust persecution and which ones had indeed committed war crimes and were trying to avoid their 'just desserts.'

"What these applicants did not realize was that I had a ready and reliable counsel. Pierre-Henri Teitgen, who served for a period as Minister of Justice, had been caught and tortured by the Gestapo before he escaped to become the greatest of the Resistance fighters. He was also one of our closest friends. I would pass the names of dubious candidates to him, and he would advise me as to their legitimacy. For the many who had clean slates, the embassy would speed their applications. For some who did not, I could assure them that, if they preferred to stay in France, the charges laid against them posed no threat and could easily be refuted.

"Others, however, were fleeing their 'just desserts,' and on Teitgen's advice I would tell them, 'Turn yourself in and you'll likely get no more than three months in prison.' For worse cases, I would simply say 'Go into hiding.'

"I would like to be able to say we never erred. But once we did: a man named Bernonville sent his wife to me claiming he had been accused of crimes he had not committed. Teitgen examined the evidence available at the time and agreed that he was innocent of any major crime. So the Embassy sent him on his way.

"But in time much more came to light, implicating him in the betrayal and deaths of many Resistance workers. Proceedings were launched in Canada to deport him to France, but he had allies in Canada who also thought him innocent; he thus managed to escape to South America. In a way, justice was served: we learned that he died there soon after he arrived."

Not all refugees, of course, admitted who they were. Pauline remembers one unusual case. "When the small French town of Vittel was liberated in the final days of the war, military authorities informed the embassy that two young women who had been imprisoned there claimed to be Canadian. Not surprisingly, they had no identification papers.

"I got there as quickly as possible, and found two haggard, emaciated girls who had been in France as students when the Germans invaded. They had been caught and imprisoned for the entire war and had not been given any food for the last two weeks of their captivity.

"I soon established that they were indeed Canadians, and we sent telegrams to their families in Canada that night. But they told me there was another Canadian in prison whom the French had not mentioned. He was from Montreal, and had been held in the cell next to them. Of course I asked to speak to him. The army authorities agreed, and said that if I was sure of his identity they would hand him over to my care.

"This man spoke perfect English, and fair Québécois. But my suspicions were aroused by the vagueness of his answers and by the fact he looked so well fed. We checked by cable with those he claimed were his parents in Canada, and they denied having any such son. Although it turned out that he had once been in Canada as an exchange student, he was in fact German, had deserted the German army and arranged to have himself held in the jail as a Canadian when the Allied armies approached.

"Had he deserted the army on moral grounds, I would have had some sympathy for him. But it turned out he had been involved in atrocities during the war, and was merely an opportunist, looking after himself when it was clear the Germans were losing."

When Georges Vanier was not engrossed in the agonies of France's rebirth, he was arranging with his army colleagues to visit Canadian forces on the front lines. Pauline often accompanied him, calling on army hospitals to talk to the wounded. One hair-raising visit was to the newly-liberated Belgian city of Antwerp.

"We were warned that explosions of unknown origin were still rocking the city, but we shrugged off the danger and insisted on going anyway. Our car had just pulled up to a makeshift downtown hospital set up in a house, when a huge blast a hundred yards away shattered half of its windows. The ground shook, the car shook, I shook. The matron of the hospital implored us to leave before other blasts occurred. She said no one could explain their origin, and that they exploded without any of the usual warnings such as the shriek of a falling aerial bomb or the rumble of artillery shells.

"Although we insisted on completing our visit, another blast, even closer to the hospital, shook the building from roof to cellar. We were horrified. First-aid workers came running into the hospital carrying stretchers, some with two or three injured and maimed civilians on each."

Only then did Pauline and her companions learn what was happening. The Germans had just developed the V-2 — a powerful, long-range rocket bomb that travelled faster than the speed of sound and gave no warning of its approach. Although originally designed to reach targets in Britain, these were aimed at newly liberated Antwerp in what was, essentially, an act of spite.

"While we completed our visit in safety, we incurred some injuries of our own as we drove out of town. Georges received a very deep cut and lost a considerable amount of blood; I was badly shaken up, had two broken ribs and could hardly breathe. I was jealous of Georges, however, because it was he who got the blood transfusions and all the sympathy, while I was told I was lucky to have come out of it with such little harm!"

Pauline also undertook many such missions on her own. One was to the town of Royan, a seaport near Bordeaux where the German garrison chose to make a last stand. "The French forces asked for help from the Canadian Red Cross, so a girl from the French Red Cross and I drove down together. We had hardly arrived in the region when it became obvious that something was happening. I was taken to see many hospitals and hostels and had lunch at a soldiers' mess. I was introduced by their commandant as the Canadian ambassador's wife. To my surprise, they muttered their disapproval and turned their backs on me. Not one to be rebuffed without knowing why, I left the commandant's table to join another where the most militant among them were concentrated. After an exchange of superficialities, I asked them point blank why they seemed to resent my presence. 'You are not one of us,' said their spokesman bluntly. I pointed out that Georges was as much a soldier as they, and had given a leg fighting for France's freedom in the First World War.

"'But you are not one of us, the workers, and when the war is over you will turn against us,' their spokesman added. 'You will renew the same oppression of us as before, although it will be we who will have won the war for you.' Suddenly the light dawned: these men had been won over by communist propaganda, as had many Resistance workers, and had been taught to believe that everyone who was not one of them was secretly against them."

Pauline and the soldiers talked for an hour, and finally parted on good terms. But the soldiers' blind faith in their beliefs was a worrying portent of how disruptive the French communist party would become in the years ahead.

"We had planned to stay overnight, but were firmly told we should leave. I was very depressed because I thought we had failed to convince them we were on their side. On the contrary, their reluctance to keep us showed a genuine concern for our welfare, because the next morning at dawn they made their final attack on the town. Their camp, where we had stayed, came under heavy gunfire, and several of them were killed. But by the end of the day, Royan had been liberated."

If gratitude was unreasonably muted in Royan, it was beyond all expectation in cities such as Caen which had been devastated, not by German, but by Canadian bombing and artillery fire. The locals who had survived the attack decked the ruins of their town in Canadian flags and bunting in appreciation of their liberators.

"We arrived in complete darkness but the next morning we could see how devasted that town was. Everything was rubble and the smell of dead bodies was so strong we had to put handkerchiefs to our noses. The prefecture was half demolished and, miraculously, the only buildings untouched were two wonderful churches. In the afternoon, we were driven right through the part that had been completely destroyed and crowds of people came out from cellars where they were living like rats and cheered us wildly. 'Vive le Canada! Vive nos libérateurs!' It was so moving. And they kept repeating to us: 'We know you had no choice but to bombard our town because the Germans used it as a stronghold. We will never forget that you gave your lives to free us.' We received the same sort of reception everywhere else we went — in Grenoble, in Lyons — everywhere people were delirious in their affection for Canada."

France's post-liberation atmosphere of exultation and recrimination, turmoil and restoration was to last at least a year. By 1947, Pauline observed: "Today I have been able to put away my Red Cross uniform and begin to live as an ambassador's wife should. De Gaulle has retreated from power, and his one-time supporters have turned coats or shuffled away into obscurity. Georges is overworked and understaffed at the embassy, so I help out there every day, needless to say without pay!" She was able to retain a small office at the embassy which she turned into an unofficial centre for Canadian students in Paris who came in droves to see her. "I didn't really do much for them except give the kind of advice only the old can give the young!"

It wasn't long before both Vaniers were thrust into the busy life of the embassy world. "We entertained continuously, and were on good terms with most major political, intellectual, artistic and business figures of France. The papal nuncio was, by virtue of his office, the official dean of the foreign diplomatic corps, but Georges had been ambassador longer than any other, so most considered him 'doyen.' Either way, I was 'doyenne,' with all the obligations that entailed.

"But every Thursday I held sacred: I would retreat for the day to my 'little oasis,' the Carmelites, to recharge my spiritual batteries. How could I get by without these gentle and unworldly sisters?"

It was also in 1947 that the Vaniers had another visit from Philippe Leclerc. "He said he would shortly be leaving for Morocco and came to say good-bye. I remember he put his arm around my shoulder and said to Georges and me: 'If anything happens to me, I leave my wife Thérèse and my children in your care.' I said, 'Philippe, how could you say such a thing when you have been through so much?' He just laughed and said, 'Well, you never know...' He went upstairs to say good-bye to Michel and then left.

"The next morning, Georges and I went to Mass and Philippe's wife Thérèse was there. She said over and over, 'I don't know why but I am so worried.' We invited her back to the house for a meal and she left at about 8:00 p.m. Then, at 11:00 p.m., René Pleven, then a member of the French cabinet, and later Prime Minister, called to deliver the most chilling news: Philippe Leclerc had been killed that day in a plane crash in the Sahara.

"Pleven came to fetch me to go with him to tell Thérèse. The two younger children were with her and I remember the first thing she did was to kneel down and say: 'Children, the only thing we can say is thank God for having given us such a wonderful father.' Then she asked Monsieur Pleven and me to take her to tell the wives of the 11 others who were killed.

"It was a time of great tension in Paris. There was a general strike and many wondered about the wisdom of having a state funeral at this time. But Georges was one who thought it might help save the day. So they went ahead.

"The night before the funeral, Philippe's body was brought into Paris, much the same way his division had entered liberated Paris. It was a foggy night and the bells were tolling and we sat with his wife and children in Les Invalides as they moved his body into the courtyard.

"The next day, there was such a moving funeral in Notre-Dame Cathedral. Hundreds of people turned out and you could have heard a pin drop during that service. You certainly would never have guessed there was a general strike! Then Philippe's coffin was carried through Paris with Thérèse and the children walking behind, and he was laid to rest in Les Invalides. My, his death was such a terrible tragedy!"

By 1953, after almost 10 years sharing in the tumultuous rebirth of France, the time came for the Vaniers to leave Paris. "By then Georges was 65 but he had no wish to retire and was certain that God would give him strength to continue to serve his country. External Affairs suggested he become ambassador to Spain or Switzerland, but Georges felt that either post would appear such a demotion in French eyes and would be taken to mean a repudiation of all his work in Paris, particularly of his unfailing support for de Gaulle."

Normally, Georges would happily have taken a posting in London, equal to Paris in prestige, and a recognition of his ability to represent Canada and all Canadians in each of its two motherlands. But the new Canadian Prime Minister, Louis St. Laurent, felt that, with a French Canadian as head of government in Ottawa at a time of resurgent Quebec nationalism, the appointment of a French Canadian to London might give the British an inaccurate signal of Canadian intentions. Georges had to agree, so the prospect of the oblivion of retirement loomed.

"At least we went out with a bang," Pauline laughed. "We gave a dinner at the embassy for some 68 people. They were all former members of the Resistance or followers of de Gaulle, and, though many were now at odds with each other, all of them accepted. I have never seen so emotional an evening. Tough old soldiers were in tears to be reunited, politicians who arrived with daggers drawn were embracing their old comrades-in-arms. For one final evening we relived the fellowship of war and the euphoria of liberation."

Georges Bidault, who had been both a Resistance hero and a Gaullist prime minister, was overcome by the event and announced that, since he could not award the *Légion d'Honneur* to Georges Vanier (Canadian diplomats cannot accept foreign honours), he would therefore award it to Pauline. "But the Canadian government said I could only receive it on the train platform as we left the station. I refused to do that, so, the morning we left Paris, Georges Bidault invited me to the Quai d'Orsay and presented it to me there. It was such a moving ceremony."

Suddenly, it was all over. The Vaniers were to leave quietly by the midnight train to Lausanne, Switzerland. But as Pauline remembers, it was anything but quiet: "I'll never forget the scene: all of our servants were wailing, and our maid, who was a Basque from Biarritz, stood on the staircase and sang *Ave Maria* in Basque. Luckily, it was New Year's Eve, or I'm sure we'd all have been run in for disturbing the peace!

"A friend who saw us off later wrote to say that he thought Georges looked so morose as he boarded the train, as if 1953 was marking the end of his useful life. And it's true, he was sad. He had so hoped to be able to continue serving his country in some capacity, however humble."

Pope John XXIII gave the Vaniers an hour-long private audience. Mme Vanier called the audience "one of the most wonderful experiences of my life."

(National Archives of Canada, PA 183618.)

The Vaniers at Vézelay, on the eve of Georges Vanier's appointment as Canada's first French-Canadian Governor General in 1959. From l to r: Thérèse, Jean, Pauline, Michel, Bernard, Georges. Byngsie, the eldest son, is absent.

(National Archives of Canada, PA 185496)

12
Retirement in Montreal
(1953-1959)

The Vaniers eased slowly into retirement. After three months in Switzerland they travelled to Venice to visit their old friend Cardinal Angelo Roncalli, the former Apostolic Nuncio in Paris who was now Patriarch of Venice. He spoke of Venice as his "retirement posting,"too modest to imagine he would later be elected Pope John XXIII, and initiate the historic Vatican II.

The Vaniers also enjoyed two months at their favourite spiritual hideaway, the hill-top town of Vézelay, near Dijon, then called on another old friend, Charles de Gaulle, now in retirement at his home in Colombey-les-Deux-Eglises in Lorraine.

In the late spring of 1954, Georges and Pauline finally sailed back to Montreal where they began a new life. They lived simply in a modest eighth-floor apartment on Sherbrooke Street, did not drive a car and devoted much of their time to helping families in the slums of Montreal.

For Georges particularly, the transition was difficult. "Georges had a hard time adjusting to a life which seemed so much less useful than did the previous 50 years. He was made a director of the Crédit Foncier and the Bank of Montreal, but these took little of his time. He had no hobbies, no special interests to pursue and so he became very depressed. I think as a result of all this his heart started giving him trouble and he also had to undergo two hernia operations. His suffering made me suffer. If only we knew at the time just how much this period was a spiritual preparation for what was to come.

"We had no real expectation of any further role in our country's life. Once in that period, we were invited to a luncheon for a member of the Queen's entourage. Someone remarked how well the first Canadian-born Governor General, Vincent Massey, was fulfilling his duties, and I mused out loud that it would be wonderful if some day a French Canadian could be named to the post. I had not even been thinking of Georges when I made the remark, but if I had been, the royal personage's answer would have put any illusions firmly to rest: 'Oh,' came the reply, 'you'll have to wait at least twenty-five years for *that*!'"

Retirement at least provided an opportunity — the first ever, except for holidays — for the Vaniers to give their undivided attention to their five children. "My, how we regretted those long years of war that so often prevented them from being with us."

Pauline Vanier was immensely proud of her children and missed no occasion to sing their praises. "By 1954, Thérèse was 31. She had risen to the rank of captain in the CWAC, worked as liaison officer in Paris, and was awarded the *Croix de Guerre* by the French government. At war's end, she left the Corps to take up medical studies, first at the Sorbonne, then at Cambridge."

Thérèse graduated from Cambridge, then interned at St. Thomas's Hospital and later at the Children's Hospital in London. There, she decided to specialize in haemotology, or studies of the blood, and eventually joined the staff of St. Thomas's Hospital in London.

"On a sabbatical at Makerere College in Uganda, she did pioneering work analysing local blood conditions, then returned to London as Senior Lecturer in St. Thomas's department of haemotology. She was the first woman to be appointed as consultant physician at the hospital.

"Byngsie, in 1954, was 29. Very reluctantly, we had sent Byngsie and the other children to Canada for the duration of the war, where they lived with my mother. After he finished Loyola College in Montreal, Byngsie joined the Canadian army, completed his training as an infantry lieutenant and was in the first cadres of the Canadian Army Pacific Force at their training school in Fort Benning, Georgia. His unit was about to leave for the Pacific when the atomic bombs brought an abrupt end to the war.

"Byngsie was now free to follow what he felt was his true vocation, a religious calling. After making a retreat at the Trappist Monastery in Oka, Quebec, he felt immediately called to this order. But first, he came to live with us in Paris for a year while he thought over his decision. We weren't too surprised when he left to join the Trappists.

"Byngsie's apprenticeship at Oka was not an easy one. After his ordination, he became terribly ill with tuberculosis, and he had to spend two years in a sanatorium before he could resume the rigours of Trappist life. Perhaps this suffering was a means of spiritual purification, for he emerged from his ordeal the most joyous man and one of great serenity."

Bernard, their second son, had plannned a career in the foreign service, but after completing his political science studies at university in Paris, he turned to painting. "Bernard gradually came to realize that painting was his calling, even though he had never taken a formal lesson. He went to live in Canada and painted in the hills north of Montreal. He then returned to France and settled first at Aix-en-Provence in a modest Provençal cottage looking out on the towering

Mont Ste-Victoire. He married a girl from Aix, and they had two lovely daughters, Valérie and Laurence. He now lives in the village of Marcoussis, south of Paris, where he has also worked as an English teacher and a translator.

"But I hope he will never stop painting: I feel he is never happier than when he is at his easel — nowhere is he better able to express the boundless beauty that is within him."

Jean, who was 26 in 1954, had continued in the navy until 1950, serving in HMCS *Magnificent,* the Canadian Navy's largest vessel.

"But Jock was having misgivings about the usefulness of a naval career in peacetime. So he studied philosophy and theology at the Institut Catholique in Paris before accepting an offer to teach philosophy at St. Michael's College in Toronto. Then, suddenly, to our dismay, he came and told us he was leaving for France to start work with the mentally handicapped.

"So off he went and it was not long before he had bought a little house in the village of Trosly, recruited a friend to help out as cook, and invited Raphael and Philippe, two young men with mental handicaps, to join him. And that was the beginning of l'Arche.

"L'Arche has now spread all over the world and Jock travels constantly, helping to nurture new communities, and giving talks and retreats in many different countries. I am truly amazed at his powers of communication. People tell me that if you hear Jock speak, you seldom leave unmoved."

Finally to Michel, born thirteen years after Jock, Pauline recalls: "I never dreamt I could have a child at 43, but how proud and happy I was when Michel arrived! But the war was reaching its fiercest, and it made me so terribly sad to leave him in Canada for the duration. He went three full years without seeing us, brought up in Montreal by my wonderfully indulgent mother who simply adored him.

"After the war, we felt the turmoil of Paris and of our own diplomatic life was no environment for a young child. We wanted him to have a Canadian education, but decided first to enroll him in a Benedictine school near Vézelay. When we returned to Canada, we found another good school in Ottawa which tried — not entirely successfully — to accommodate the difference in standards between a European and a North American education.

"Michel then went to a highly recommended Swiss school in Fribourg, which turned out to be a strict and austere place. But he graduated with distinction, returned to Canada at 17, and entered Laval University to study philosophy. Before long, he enlisted as an officer in his father's old regiment, the Royal 22nd, in its most demanding branch, the paratrooper batallion.

"It took a lot of courage to complete that two-year ordeal, but he did so with honour. He then returned to university, took a master's degree in political science and, upon graduation, took up a post as professor of political science at a Montreal 'CEGEP,' or community college. He married and has two delightful children, Anne-Marie and Philippe.

"It has not been an easy life for any of our children, but oh my, I am so proud of each one of them."

In 1957, in an overwhelming landslide, the Progressive Conservatives, led by John Diefenbaker, took power in Canada for the first time in 22 years. "If the Royal comments about the unlikelihood of a French Canadian becoming Governor General had not been enough to discourage us," Pauline confided, "a Conservative victory certainly seemed to be a nail in the coffin. Mr. Diefenbaker and Georges had never met, much less come to know each other. Although Georges had been meticulous in his duty as a civil servant not to be partisan in any way, his diplomatic appointments had all been made by Liberal regimes; Mackenzie King regarded Georges almost as his protégé, and Mike Pearson, our great friend from London days, had now become leader of the Liberal party which was now in opposition."

Georges was therefore more curious than startled when, in April 1959, John Diefenbaker invited him to Ottawa for a chat. "For several minutes," Pauline learned from Georges, "the Prime Minister beat around the bush making only superficial conversation. Then he came to the subject of governors general, how one would need to be appointed soon to replace Vincent Massey, and how he had several candidates in mind, none of them a French Canadian.

"'But,' the Prime Minister continued, '1959 is the 200th anniversary of the Battle of the Plains of Abraham, which sealed the conquest of New France by the British. Perhaps we should have a French-Canadian governor general to underline the fact that 1759 has long since become more of a partnership than a conquest. And besides,' Diefenbaker added, 'although we hardly know each other, you come very highly recommended. . . . In short, would you, Georges, like the job?'

"Georges rushed back to Montreal to tell me the news, and ask my advice. But I could see he had already made up his mind. I asked him, 'At 71, don't you think you should first have another medical check-up? After all, you have had two heart attacks, minor though they were.' His answer was magnificent. 'No,' he said, 'if I'm meant to do this job, God will give me the strength. I don't need to consult any doctors.' And he didn't, until his last days in office.

"The Lord certainly did give him strength. From that moment on, he was rejuvenated in mind, body and spirit. Gone were the five years of relative idleness and depression, of minor ailments magnified into major ones, of spiritual emptiness. For the next seven years Georges was to have the heart of a 20-year-old."

The Vaniers faced the difficult task, however, of keeping Georges' appointment a secret from that April until the date of its announcement in August. Rumours were rampant, so maintaining secrecy was not easy. The Queen came to Canada in June to present colours to the Royal 22nd, but neither she nor Georges had a moment to themselves to discuss the appointment.

Nor could Georges confide to his old friend Cardinal Roncalli, when he, as the newly elected Pope John XXIII, received the Vaniers and Jock at the Vatican that summer.

The visit turned out to be a memorable one. "It was the most moving encounter. He took each of us in his arms and embraced us so warmly, then said, 'Remember, I'm still Roncalli. I'm still the same Roncalli. But now I'm the Vicar of Christ and it is a very heavy burden. I need your prayers.'"

Pope John gave them a private audience in his library that lasted a full hour, which Pauline fondly remembers. "It was one of the most wonderful experiences of my life. Then Georges, in his excitement, completely forgot protocol and boldly asked His Holiness if we could attend his private Mass the next morning, something you really should never do. And he said, 'Why not?' So the next morning, we were up at 5:00 a.m. and reached the Vatican by 6:30 a.m. We were met by Guido, His Holiness's valet, who took us up in an elevator and showed us to the Pope's private chapel, no bigger than a small room. Two little nuns were the only others there and his private secretary was serving Mass. It was so beautiful.

"One thing was very touching. There was no altar rail, so to kneel down you had to get right down to the floor without any support. Just before prayers began, His Holiness remembered about Georges' leg and asked his valet to bring over a *prie-dieu* so that Georges could use it. Isn't that charming? Just imagine that we were the first lay people ever to attend his private Mass!

"After the prayers were over, he asked us to go out with him. He said he would like to give us breakfast, but it is just not done. He would like us, however, to stay and talk. So we remained for an hour and a quarter! Every time we got up to leave — we made about ten attempts — he would say, 'Encore un moment, encore un moment.'

"Then he took us to his bedroom, proudly showed us a photograph of his mother, 'La bonne Mama,' and passed it to each of us to kiss. His room was very simple: a bed, a little table, an old desk. He showed us the big window that overlooks St. Peter's Square. On an impulse, I went to look outside, but His Holiness quickly asked me to keep out of sight: 'I can't imagine how many rumours we would start if people in the square below saw a *woman* peering out of the Pope's bedroom!'

"When we were finally about to leave, he came right out to the lift with us and we knelt down and he gave us the last blessing and put his arms around Jock's neck. As you can imagine, we were terribly saddened by his death a few years later. Every time we go back to Rome, we visit his grave in St. Peter's and it is always piled high with flowers. My, how the people adored that man!"

The official announcement of the Vanier's appointment was to be made in early August, and they were supposed to be informed privately by telegram well ahead of time. It was not to be. "The crucial telegram went astray, and we never received it. We were in London with Michel, staying in a tiny room at the Rembrandt Hotel on the afternoon of August 1, and Georges had gone to a late Mass while I did some errands. We arrived back at the hotel together to find Michel beside himself with excitement. 'Daddy's been named the new Governor General!' he said. He had heard by a phone call from the High Commission.

"The hotel insisted we move to a larger room, and the telephone started ringing off the hook with friends calling to congratulate us. Nonetheless, we decided to go ahead with our original plans to see the film *The Nun's Story*. All the way, we were badgered by the press who could not imagine that on the evening of such an announcement we would be doing anything so mundane as seeing a movie. They thought we should be drinking champagne at Claridge's!

"We kept our reservations back to Canada by ship and, when we docked in Quebec, there was an urgent message waiting for us: Could we proceed to Ottawa immediately to rehearse the upcoming ceremonies for taking office? Suddenly, I realized we were back into a life which would likely be as hectic as any we had left in Paris five years before."

The vice-regal couple jumped into their new life with an energy and fervour that characterized their whole term.

(National Archives of Canada, PA 185492.)

13
Government House, Ottawa (1959-1967)

Few Governor General appointments — before or since — have created such interest. English and French newspapers, both in Canada and Europe, carried headlines applauding the choice of the distinguished soldier/diplomat as the country's second Canadian-born Governor General and the first French Canadian to hold the post. When the Vaniers arrived back in Canada in early September 1959, there was a palpable atmosphere of excitement over their impending investiture, scheduled for September 15.

They both approached the installation ceremony with trepidation. "The day before, the Secretary of State met us in Montreal and accompanied us by train to Ottawa. Prime Minister and Mrs. Diefenbaker greeted us at the station, and presented the ministers of Cabinet. I remember saying to Mr. Diefenbaker: 'Mr. Prime Minister, although we've never met, you have offered to take us both on, and me sight unseen. Now that I'm here, you are still free to change your mind!'" Her offer was met with laughter and applause, and set the tone for the cordial and informal relations that endured throughout their term of office.

Always down to earth, Mme Vanier cheers up two Inuit patients in the Inuvik General
Hospital, Inuvik, NWT, 1961.

The Vaniers spent the night in the Chateau Laurier Hotel. "It was wonderful. We were given a whole floor for all our friends and relatives. And when our old friend Abbé Leclerc arrived the next morning to say Mass in our room, he discovered that Georges had been up since dawn, writing and rewriting his inaugural speech. Georges was getting so discouraged that he had rung up a friend to ask his help in polishing the wording. But his friend said he must decline: the speech, he said, must be pure Vanier, and if it were, anything he could add would be superfluous."

The day of the installation dawned and, at 10:00 a.m., Vincent Massey, the departing Governor General, left Ottawa and the ceremony of the installation of Canada's nineteenth Governor General began.

The Vaniers arrived at Parliament Hill by car to the salute of a hundred-man honour guard and entered the Senate Chamber for the glittering ceremony. They were a striking couple: the tall white-haired Vanier in his much-decorated military uniform and Pauline, regal and stately, with a white bouquet offsetting her simple black taffeta gown. "The whole thing unfolded in the most wonderful atmosphere of joy and celebration. And Georges' speech was vintage Vanier. I felt we were off to a promising start."

Following the ceremony, a 21-gun salute was fired from Nepean Point, the Governor General's flag was raised on the Peace Tower, and the vice-regal couple mounted an open state landau for the ride through downtown Ottawa. Escorted by a troop of scarlet-coated mounted police, they rode to the steps of Government House. "It felt a little like a homecoming," Pauline said, recalling her earlier stay as a young bride in Rideau Cottage just 200 yards across the lawn. "Georges once said that while he claimed he was never handicapped by his wooden leg, it took him 37 years to get from Rideau Cottage to Government House!"

The vice-regal couple jumped into their new life with an energy and fervour that characterized their whole term. They had barely unpacked when they welcomed their first visitor, Princess Alice, widow of the Earl of Athlone who had been Governor General from 1940 to 1946. "On the first day of her visit, I asked her if she would give me a briefing. I said to her, 'I haven't got any blue blood and I don't have a *clue* how to behave in this job.'

"So we installed ourselves in my sitting room and she started. 'First you must at all times appear slightly aloof and keep a little distance. And never let people call you 'Pauline.' You must be prepared for people who will curtsy to you. And on no account must you embrace anyone in public, specially a political figure, lest it show favouritism.' I found all this very difficult, given my character."

Nonetheless, she set out to follow Princess Alice's precepts. "The next day, we held our first major reception. It was for veterans of the Canadian Army's artillery forces. Their wives were also included, and curtsying was still in order. But when the first woman was presented to me, I completely forgot my new role and found myself curtsying to her. So we clashed kneecaps on the way down!"

There was more to come that would shock Princess Alice. "Right at the end of the receiving line, I spotted the beaming face of my old friend Mike Pearson, then leader of the opposition. I was so delighted to see him that without thinking I threw my arms around his neck and kissed him warmly."

She later confessed her sin to Princess Alice who was scandalized. "She told me that, as just punishment, I must now kiss Mr. Diefenbaker as well. It was the Christmas season before I had a chance. I hardly knew Mr. Diefenbaker well enough to initiate anything myself, so I stood under some mistletoe and looked expectantly at him. I waited and waited but he didn't take the hint. Then I caught his wife's eye, and she realized my predicament at once. 'John,' she said, 'don't you see Her Excellency is standing under the mistletoe?' Happily, the prime minister rose gallantly to the occasion and obliged. I had done my penance."

Before long, the Vaniers' life fell into a busy, active pattern. Their social obligations alone would have exhausted anyone half their ages. In their first year in office, they entertained over 10,000 people in an almost never-ending round of luncheons and dinners, receptions and teas. Children were their favourite visitors — Boy Scouts and Girl Guides, school patrollers and sea cadets and, every Christmas, the 200 underprivileged youngsters of the Ottawa Boys' Club. On these raucous occasions, both Vaniers would don paper hats and pull firecrackers with the wildest of them.

No matter what lay ahead of them, the Vaniers began every day by attending Mass together, usually in the small chapel they installed in an upstairs bedroom. "It was the first time Government House had a chapel and that little room came to mean so much to us. And on Sundays, we went to different churches around Ottawa. This way we touched a real cross section of the city. And the reception we were given! My, it was touching!"

Staff get-togethers were also a special joy to Pauline Vanier who, like her husband, took a keen personal interest in every member, regarding them as an extension of their own family. She referred to most of them as "my adopted children," invited them often to share meals with them, and carried them hot bouillon when they were sick. Said one: "I don't know how she had the energy to care so much for so many people. My God, how she cared!" But it all came quite naturally to Pauline Vanier. "It was such a wonderful happy family, wasn't it? And didn't we have some crazy times together?"

One of those crazy times was a costume party they gave for the staff. With the party in full swing, the two Vaniers, dressed up as a pair of work horses, with a leather harness slung around their shoulders, clip-clopped into the ballroom pulling a sleigh, with

141

Pauline Vanier leading the charge. "She came galloping in, pawing the air and snorting like a horse," recalled aide-de-camp Bruce Stock. "Every time she reached up, she would tug on the reins and nearly topple over the Governor General."

Though Pauline Vanier was stimulated by her non-stop social obligations, she was determined to find time to do more. "I did enjoy the life, but I wanted to do more for people who needed help." Whether in Ottawa or on her travels, she seized any opportunity to visit men's and women's prisons, homes for children or the handicapped, hostels and hospitals. As one Ottawan put it: "Pauline Vanier can make any sick child happy just by patting him on the head and saying, 'Everything will soon be all right.'"

She insisted on answering most of her own mail — as many as 50 letters a day were addressed to her personally — and often penned replies in her own hand or typed them herself on her ancient portable typewriter. "Most of my letters are from women with problems. I am so deeply touched by the trust they have in me. I feel the least I can do is answer them myself."

She did just that, often with more than just sympathy. When letters complained of an injustice, she found herself acting, as did Georges, in a role never assigned to them nor expected of them: that of informal ombudsmen.

By exercising their right to be informed, both Vaniers would send messages to the authorities in question, noting the alleged injustice. This was usually enough to jolt a complacent bureaucrat into investigating the complaint. "It gave me so much satisfaction when I could do something to help correct an injustice. Some of these people had been suffering for years."

Pauline Vanier, however, shouldered her own share of suffering. For almost 30 years, she had been troubled by incipient cataracts and her sight was becoming so clouded that she had to rely more and more on sound and intuition to recognize guests, as well as discreet guidance to avoid running into obstacles. Her courage in insisting on fulfilling all her duties under such circumstances amazed her staff and friends. "I knew an operation might cure me. But I was told that in my case it might equally well make things worse, so I kept putting it off."

Finally, one incident convinced her she was being more foolish than brave. "We were standing on the back platform of our train as we left a small town we had visited when I saw what I thought was a playground full of children. I waved to them vigorously and wondered why they seemed to stand fixed to the ground and not wave back. 'Your Excellency,' one of my aides told me gently, 'there is no need to wave: that is a graveyard we are passing.' We doubled up with laughter over that one. But at least it made me decide to undergo the operation immediately."

She admitted the operation was a terrifying experience. "I was given only a local anesthetic, and remained awake throughout. Somehow, I felt as if the scalpels were scraping at my innermost soul! To distract myself, I began reciting A.A. Milne — 'Christopher Robin goes hoppity, hoppity . . .' I kept on reciting until it was all over.

"But oh, the joy to be able to see again! After I was discharged, I went straight to the greenhouse at Government House and found I could see perfectly the smallest, most delicate flowers. And specially the *white* ones — I had never seen the white ones before. I just screamed with joy! For the first time since coming to Government House I saw those dear little white impatiens. I think that's why I became so attached to the flowers at Government House. They gave me more joy than I can say.

"I also felt I wanted everyone to have more beauty around them. So I managed to persuade the government to refurbish and redecorate all the staff quarters and servants' rooms and secretaries' offices. Some of them hadn't been touched since the last century! After we did over the ballroom, I finally had a sense of belonging to that house."

When Pauline Vanier was not helping to run the vast 50-room mansion and sumptuous gardens of Government House, supervising a staff of 25 or handling the exhausting entertainment obligations, she joined her husband on travels that covered several thousand kilometres each year and took them into large and small communities in every corner of the land. She loved these trips and found them infinitely rewarding.

"It was the best way to keep in touch with the mood across the country. Nearly always, we received such wonderful receptions wherever we went. It was only in British Columbia that we encountered, and then only at first, any obvious hostility. I can remember the Premier wasn't sure if he liked having a French Canadian as Governor General. The population wasn't sure either. Our second visit was much better: people had discovered we weren't too bad after all, I guess. I'm not sure we ever won over Premier Bennett, but we made many good friends in B.C., and subsequently were always warmly welcomed.

"It's strange how often Canadians have the impression that the Governor General is just another politician, no matter how neutral we attempted to be. I only strayed from that once: the time I came close to making any sort of political statement when I declined to help open the Calgary Stampede. Not only was I too old but I was espousing the cause of the Indians and they are so resentful of the stampede. They found someone else to do the honours."

If their travel schedule was arduous, so too was the succession of distinguished visitors the Vaniers welcomed to Government House. Each one brought his or her own portfolio of memories. General de Gaulle came with his wife long before his momentous 1967 visit to

Canada, and gave no hint of the havoc he would wreak on the subsequent occasion, when he endorsed Quebec's independence movement.

On every visit, no personal touch was forgotten. "I always liked to leave some carefully selected books in their rooms," Pauline noted. "For General de Gaulle, I concentrated on recent Canadian literature in French. But when I was making a last-minute check, I realized all the books I had left for him were printed in the European fashion, with all the pages uncut. So I sat down and went through each volume cutting the pages free."

Because Charles de Gaulle was occupied with meetings, it was his wife, Yvonne, whom Pauline came to know even better on that occasion. "I asked her if she would like to go for a drive in the country, but she said, 'No, I am one who spends my time in waiting. I've never been able to be much use to my husband, but I'm always there when he comes back. The only other thing I do well for him is to butter his bread at breakfast.'

"She was a noble woman in her humility, always in the background, but always there. Do you realize she *never* left his side throughout the war? In all those years, she also had to look after their mentally-handicapped child, particularly difficult during their impoverished years in England. The poor child died at age 17. That was the last time I saw them in Canada and they couldn't have been nicer."

The visit in May 1961 by the recently elected U.S. President, John F. Kennedy, and his wife, Jacqueline, was memorable for the massive phalanx of security men and equipment that accompanied them. Several hundred U.S. secret servicemen and federal agents and hundreds of crates of electronic equipment preceded them to Ottawa. "I've never seen so much security. Our entire internal telephone system was taken over and when I lifted the receiver to call Mrs. Kennedy in her room down the hall, an operator in Washington

Pauline Vanier struck up an instant rapport with Farah, wife of the Shah of Iran.

(National Archives of Canada, PA 185491.)

answered and demanded to know who I was and why I wanted to call the President's wife!

"Finally, Georges threw all the F.B.I. and C.I.A. men out of the building and had them replaced by well-indoctrinated RCMP officers. Even that made little difference, however. For example, when I went to visit Jacqueline Kennedy in her room, I was stopped at her door by two hulking RCMP plainclothes men who wouldn't let me pass! When we finally got together, I was a little mischievous when I said to the RCMP officer: 'You might be interested to know who we two suspicious characters are — this is Mrs. Jacqueline Kennedy and my name is Pauline Vanier!'"

The Vaniers also received several heads of state from Latin American countries. One visit, that of the President of Argentina, caused the greatest uproar when their embassy in Ottawa managed to lose all the luggage belonging to the President and his entourage.

Pauline laughs as she recalls the occasion: "Both the president and his wife had arrived in casual travelling clothes, and we were giving them a formal state dinner within the hour. The president's wife was tiny, and none of us had anything that would fit her, so she had to wear one of my large dresses turned up with safety pins. The president, by contrast, was huge, so our long-legged son Michel provided trousers that almost fitted him. But the biggest jacket we could find didn't come within a foot of buttoning in front!

"The guests arrived, the men in white tie and tails and glittering decorations, the women in formal dresses and tiaras. Our two guests of honour never turned a hair! To their enormous credit, they pulled it off with good humour and dignity, and the dinner was a great success."

One visitor with whom Pauline struck up an instant rapport was Farah, the wife of the Shah of Iran. "She was such a strikingly beautiful woman of great intelligence and sincerity; we spent hours discussing her attempts, in the face of great conservative opposition within her adopted country, to help improve the lot of women with social reforms such as day-care centres."

Another visitor was the then Ethiopian Emperor, Haile Selassie. "He was a very small man, but one of such dignity and intelligence that he seemed tall and commanding. What completely bowled me over was the strength and simplicity of his Coptic Christian faith. 'Lion of Judah or not,' he said to me, 'all I try to be is a good telephone for the Holy Spirit.'"

Of all the memories of her seven-and-a-half-year term at Government House, one event, "the most frightening but ultimately most inspiring," stands out vividly in Pauline Vanier's memory — the visit to Quebec by Queen Elizabeth in October 1964.

"A small group of militant separatists were strongly opposed to the visit, and saw it as an opportunity to rally Quebeckers to their cause. There were even declarations that the 'Queen's safety could not be guaranteed,' a hint that an attempt might be made on her life. And there was opposition to the visit in English-speaking Canada for that reason alone. But Lester Pearson, the Prime Minister, urged that the visit should go ahead; to cancel it would give unwarranted credibility to the separatists.

"We met her when her ship, the *Britannia,* docked in Quebec and drove with her and Prince Philip through the streets of the town. It looked like a city under siege: no crowds, just police everywhere, guns cocked at the ready. When some news photographers tried to take pictures of her arrival at the Chateau Frontenac hotel, they were chased away by club-wielding policemen.

"The Queen addressed the provincial legislature and spoke eloquently in perfect French of the enormous role in the development of Canada played by French Canadians in the past and of the great contribution they can make to a united Canada in the future. She was calm and unruffled, a striking contrast to the

Quebec premier who looked flushed and agitated and spoke in a hesitant and quivering voice. I later told her how much I marvelled at her serenity in such circumstances, and she said, with a twinkle in her eye, 'Every time the politicians appear to get more nervous, I seem to get calmer.'

"Many Quebeckers were won over by the Queen on that visit. I introduced her to Réal Caouette, the leader of the Quebec Social Credit Party, and he soon had her roaring with laughter with his stories. The next day in the House of Commons, he announced that, as a result of his conversation, he had become an ardent royalist, and would henceforward be one of Her Majesty's most loyal subjects!"

As the Vaniers' term at Government House progressed, they began to discuss together what legacy they could leave behind them. One subject that had long concerned them both was the integrity of the family.

"For some time, we had been concerned about family breakdown. We were struck by the possibility that a close look at the family in Canada could help more people to find the same warm family relationships that both my husband and I have enjoyed in our own childhoods and in our own family."

Thus on June 7, 1964, they sponsored a conference at Government House that attracted 400 delegates from across the country. This led to the formation the next year of the Vanier Institute of the Family, the first such organization in the country set up to promote research on family-related matters.

That same year, Pauline Vanier's support of academic excellence resulted in her appointment as the first layperson and first woman Chancellor of the University of Ottawa, a position she retained even after Georges's death. Her installation, she confided later, was one of her proudest moments. When she stood to address the packed hall, she paused briefly, cast a momentary glance at her husband, then spoke about one of the subjects closest to her heart:

"On the university rests the crucial responsibility of expounding the Christian principles which form the essence and foundation of our Western civilization, and to show that faith — far from being old-fashioned — imparts a beauty, a richness and a radiance that can be found in no other source....Idealism comes naturally to the young, if we encourage it to flourish. But idealism without a faith to motivate and sustain it will wither when it faces the trials and temptations of adulthood. So above all else, we must cultivate faith and a sense of values in our young or our society will crumble around us."

The sudden death of Georges Vanier on March 5, 1967, saddened the entire nation. That same morning, he was alert and conscious when his faithful chaplain, Chanoine Guindon, arrived to give him Holy Communion in his room while the family attended Mass together in the chapel next door. But he slipped away quickly; Mass was followed by last rites. Characteristically, his final words to his wife and family consisted of a whimsical family joke. Pushed to superhuman limits for too many years, his gallant soldier's heart quietly and peacefully gave up.

The whole country was plunged into mourning. Almost 30,000 people filed past the Senate Chamber where Georges' flag-draped casket lay in state, while thousands more across the land paid their own personal tributes. Said his long-time secretary, Esmond Butler: "It was one of the greatest outpourings of affection ever seen on the part of Canadians."

Three days later, on March 8, in a televised ceremony that was watched by millions, Georges Vanier's coffin was carried on an oaken gun-carriage through the icy streets of Ottawa to the Notre-Dame Basilica for a full state funeral.

Later, to the muffled roll of drums, the tolling of bells and a booming 78-gun salute — one for each year of the Governor General's life — Pauline Vanier and her family left Ottawa station to accompany the coffin by train to Quebec City. Following a commemorative service in Notre-Dame Cathedral, Georges Vanier's body was laid to rest in the Royal 22nd Regiment's memorial chapel in the Citadel.

Pauline Vanier bore the long ordeals of these funeral services with courage and composure, comforted by the knowledge that her husband had served his God and his country as well as any man could. "He loved that job, and he loved the contacts with so many different Canadians. He definitely felt that this was a mission, that this was something he had been pre-ordained to do."

Tributes to the late Governor General were eloquent and moving. "He loved us — openly, and we loved him back. And that fact alone has warmed us for a century to come," said Hugh Kemp on CBC radio while Ontario's Lieutenant Governor Earl Rowe saluted Georges Vanier as "one of the outstanding men of his time." He added, "No man had a higher conception of public duty. Governor General and Pauline Vanier gave to our country a service and dignity unexcelled in the last 100 years."

But it was journalist Peter Newman who spoke most poignantly to a grieving nation. "How long is it since we, as a nation, have cried?" he wrote. "The tears were for Georges Vanier, but the sadness in part was for the end of an era. This was the funeral service for a generation."

Prime Minister Pearson contemplated asking Pauline Vanier herself to assume the office of Governor General. But in view of the heavy demands of Centennial Year, he decided it would be asking too much of someone who was still coping with a period of such great stress. She stayed on at Government House for some weeks after her husband's death, pending the arrival and installation of Roland Michener as his successor.

It was a time of sadness and reflection. Besides traumatically recasting her life, as all bereaved widows must, Pauline was determined to reply personally to many of the over 10,000 letters of condolence that poured into Government House.

Her devoted staff stayed on, though she scolded them for continuing to treat her like the vice-regal First lady. "I am no longer 'Excellency,'" she told them. "Why not just call me Ma Vanier?" And to her dignified butler, "Do please sit down, McKinnon. We're both ordinary citizens now!"

On April 13, 1967, Pauline Vanier bid farewell to her staff and walked out of the doors of Government House as First Lady for the last time. She rode to Ottawa station where Prime Minister Pearson, cabinet members, diplomats and representatives of the church and the armed forces gathered on the platform to say good-bye. After greeting each one and inspecting a guard of honour, she had a special good-bye for aide-de-camp David Hyman. As he tried to salute, his military poise was shattered when she leaned over and planted a kiss on his cheek.

She climbed aboard the train and stood on the open platform at the back waving and blowing kisses to all those left behind. Then, as the guard of honour presented arms and played a last salute, she dropped them a curtsy, and waved again as the train pulled out of the station.

It may have been the end of an era, but for Pauline Vanier it was simply the end of a chapter. Little did she know that another, completely new life would begin for her in the not-too-distant future.

14
Montreal and l'Arche: A New Chapter Begins (1967 - 1991)

Pauline Vanier moved to Montreal and settled into a small row house on Redpath Place. Her husband's devoted valet, Yves Chevrier, occupied the basement apartment to help out with household chores and many close friends and family members visited regularly to comfort her and help her through a difficult period of transition.

One of her top priorities was to transform an upstairs bedroom into a small chapel, with a black and white tile floor, a simple altar and her husband's crucifix. An Oblate priest came early every morning to say Mass and a secretary visited three mornings a week to help with the huge volume of mail that continued to arrive.

That June, her Montreal home well established, Pauline decided to travel to France to see her children and old friends. It was a time of increasingly strained relations between Canada and France. As her husband had sensed before his death, Pauline perceived that worrying changes were taking place in President de Gaulle's attitude towards Canada. The French

The all-engulfing hug was Pauline Vanier's trademark.

(L'Arche photo.)

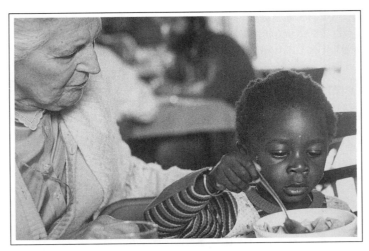

Pauline Vanier loved children and she missed no opportunity to make a new friend.

(L'Arche photo.)

president appeared to be deliberately encouraging Quebec separatism, by promoting the Quebec provincial delegation in Paris to the status of an embassy, and treating the visiting Quebec premier as if he were the head of an independent country. While Georges was puzzled by these actions, he strongly doubted that his old friend wished to break up Canada, France's faithful ally in two world wars. But Pauline was not so sure.

Pauline happened to be in Paris during a ceremony commemorating those who died in the Resistance and, when Madame de Gaulle spotted her in the crowd, she insisted Pauline greet the General. "De Gaulle shook hands with me formally. After expressing his condolences on my husband's death, he spoke of his forthcoming state visit to Canada (he was one of dozens of world leaders invited to visit during Centennial year). He then said how sad he was that we would not be receiving him in Quebec and Montreal. It was only afterwards that it dawned on me that he had not mentioned Ottawa." (State visits to any country traditionally begin in the capital.) Could it be possible the omission was merely an oversight?

"I left for London and wrote a personal letter to Madame de Gaulle thanking her for her help that day and finished it by saying I would be honoured if she would allow me to call on them before they left for Canada. I don't know what made me do this but I had this thing on my mind about de Gaulle omitting Ottawa and I just had to act.

"I received a handwritten note by return post inviting me to lunch the next week, so I went back to Paris. They sent a car for me and I arrived at the Elysée Palace and, to my great surprise, I found myself alone with the de Gaulles.

"We went into the dining room and I sat between the two. I had barely sat down when General de Gaulle turned to me and said, 'Madame Vanier, what future do you think there is for Canada?' I replied, 'General, I can think of no other future than that which my husband envisaged, a country united by two great founding races.' He dismissed my statement with a wave of his hand, and said sharply, 'Unity is out of the question — even sovereignty association is barely thinkable. Only a free and independent Quebec will be able to save North American civilization.'

"I was stunned. I told him frankly that I thought he was playing a dangerous game, that he would throw us into the arms of the Americans and that inevitably the Americans wouldn't allow either Quebec or what remained of Canada to be really independent countries. He ignored my words and went on and on about the inevitable trend of French civilization.

"After lunch, we spoke briefly but I thought it was time to go. He walked me to the car and the last thing I said was, 'Thank God my husband is not alive to hear you.' Then I got into the car and left.

"Perhaps I was wrong to have insisted on meeting with de Gaulle. But I felt I had to speak out in defence of Canada. I thought it might just help the situation between France and Canada at that time. But my, how that visit shattered me! It was so painful because of our love for France and our friendship for both de Gaulles. To this day I cannot believe that a man of his intelligence could have possibly said the things he did. Some people suspect the Quebec premier influenced him but I know he is not a man who is easily influenced. I am convinced it was his own idea. It was certainly his own decision."

She reported her conversation to the Canadian Embassy in Paris, suggesting they warn Ottawa about possible trouble on de Gaulle's forthcoming trip. It made little difference: the French President went ahead with his visit to Canada in July, and soon was comparing his motor trip from Quebec to Montreal with the liberation of Paris from German occupation. The climax of his visit, witnessed by thousands in person and millions on television, came when he stood on the balcony of Montreal's City Hall and shouted the slogan, not only of Quebec *independentists,* but also of its terrorists: *"Vive le Quebec libre!"*

The Canadian Prime Minister issued a statement regretting de Gaulle's statement and pointing out that Quebec was already free, and did not need 'liberating.' It was a mild rebuke, but de Gaulle seized upon it as the excuse he needed to cut short his visit to Canada without including Ottawa.

In France, however, it seemed the French people were tiring of their President's autocratic ways. Within a few months, students and workers were staging worse anti-government riots than had been seen for almost a century. In 1969, de Gaulle lost a constitutional referendum which would have reduced the power of the French Senate in his favour. He resigned and died the following year.

"It was a tragic end to a courageous and dedicated career," Pauline observed, "but now I know why the good Lord called Georges when He did. If his heart had not failed him in March, it would certainly not have survived those words of de Gaulle in July."

Pauline returned to Montreal and renewed her active interest in social service. She became the driving force behind the Vanier Institute of the Family, worked tirelessly to help improve Montreal slum conditions and visited and counselled prisoners.

One prisoner she came to know well was a young man named Rolland who was serving a 20-year sentence. He was due for parole and, at the request of the prison chaplain and a friend from the John Howard Society, Pauline agreed to meet him and help ease his re-entry into society.

"He would come every week for a meal and would ring me every night, between 9:00 and 10:00. I tried very hard to help him but he found it difficult to handle his new-found freedom. After several months, the phone calls stopped and I learned that he had reverted to crime, had been arrested and returned to prison.

"I continued trying to help him but it was to no avail: his return to prison made him deeply depressed and, unable to face the future, the poor man committed suicide." Pauline Vanier was among the handful of mourners who attended his funeral.

This was a time that Pauline was also called upon by the business world who sought her expertise in community and social relations. She agreed to serve as a director of the Bell Canada telephone company, the Montreal Institute of Cardiology and the Bank of Montreal. And she continued to preside over the affairs of the University of Ottawa as its Chancellor.

During this period, Pauline often journeyed to France to visit her son Jean at l'Arche, the community he founded in the village of Trosly-Breuil, northeast of Paris, for men and women with mental handicaps. She greatly enjoyed these visits, but always returned home with grave doubts that she herself could ever be a permanent part of Jean's community. To understand why, one must visit l'Arche at Trosly — or any of the over 98 such homes that now operate in 25 countries.

Trosly is not only the first community to have been created, it is also the largest. About 200 men and women with handicaps live in two dozen homes scattered through the village and four neighbouring towns. Sharing their lives are almost as many "assistants" — idealistic young people and more mature men and women from around the world who have come to l'Arche looking for some tangible purpose to their lives and a way to serve those less fortunate than themselves.

Many of the handicapped function reasonably well, in spite of wounds they have suffered from being rejected by their families and by society. Others have such severe disabilities they can barely speak or do anything for themselves. It can be difficult and disturbing to encounter them for the first time; it can even be repelling and frightening. Such reactions are common among the hundreds of the young assistants who flock to help out at l'Arche; it was no different for Pauline Vanier.

Back in Montreal, however, she was becoming increasingly restless. She resumed her previous routines, but began to feel a gnawing lack of sufficient self-giving in her life. Friends suggested a move to l'Arche might be the answer, but she was reluctant to take such a step.

"I was obviously dissatisfied with my life at the time, but I just didn't think I was up to a move to l'Arche. The emotional demands on everyone there are unbelievable. And I was no longer a young girl of twenty."

A frequent visitor at the time was Sue Mosteller, a religious sister who became International Co-ordinator for l'Arche after moving to the l'Arche community of Daybreak, north of Toronto. She recalls her visits with Pauline Vanier in her Montreal home.

"It was a time of deep anguish and soul-searching," she said. "She was plagued by so many doubts — whether she could adjust to a world so different from the one she came from, whether she could, as Jean used to say, 'step down the ladder.' She did, but it was a very big step. And she anguished about whether she could live the more interior world of l'Arche. She was very comfortable in the outer world but she had tremendous doubts about the strength of her inner, spiritual world."

Pauline also confided some of her fears to Barbara Swanekamp, an assistant who has lived at l'Arche since its inception. "She wrote to me to say she doubted that she would be able to 'fit in' with us, that she was too much of a 'bourgeois lady' to live the very simple life we do here, to find serenity in poverty or spirituality in suffering."

159

So Barbara sent her a postcard saying simply, "Come live and die with us." "She knew at once what I meant," said Barbara. "Not to 'die' physically, but to renounce material comforts and intellectual inhibitions, and to live with us in the simplicity of unrestrained love. She told me later that she treasured that postcard and glanced often at its message."

But Pauline knew she would have to make *some* change, if only to renew some purpose in her life. So early in 1970, she decided to seek help. "I was desperately looking for direction," she recalls. So she went on a retreat with "my dear little sisters," the Carmelites, in a Montreal convent.

She stayed for almost two weeks. "Every day, the sisters would ask me, 'Is there any news yet?' 'Well, no,' I'd say, 'no hard news yet.'" Then, on her last day, the Gospel reading was the parable of the rich man, who says to himself, "I have enough money for the rest of my life: I will take life easy, eat, drink and enjoy myself, and not give a damn for anyone else," to which God replies, "You fool! Tonight your soul will be required of you. How much money have you got stored up in heaven?"

"I felt struck to the quick. Suddenly, I realized how much I cherished my own materialist inclinations and style of life. Then and there, I decided to sell as many of my possessions as I could, send the proceeds to Jean and, for better or worse, move to l'Arche.

"At the time my vanity told me I was setting a good example, and I felt quite smug. But I got my proper reward: instead of praising me, most people told me I'd gone 'gaga'!"

She auctioned off much of her furniture, books and personal possessions and stepped down from her directorships. She hesitated to sell her house, however, "in case it all didn't work out and I wanted to come back." And in February 1972, at the age of 73, Pauline Vanier flew to France to begin what was to be a demanding, emotionally turbulent, and quite unpredictable new life.

She moved into a rambling wood-frame house called Les Marronniers, named for the huge chestnut tree in the garden. The house was perfect for Pauline. It was in the centre of the village, close to where Jean lived and walking distance from most of the l'Arche houses in Trosly. She lived at one end of the ground floor in an apartment-like wing with a cozy sitting room overlooking the garden, a small bedroom, a lounge-dining room and a modestly equipped but spacious kitchen. She covered the walls with vibrant paintings by her son, Bernard, packed the shelves to overflowing with her treasured books and placed photographs of her husband and children on every table.

The adjustment to life outside the oasis of her "cottage" was far from easy. While she was happy to be installed in Jean's home base, she was dismayed to discover he was so busy with commitments around the world that she would be lucky to see him once a week.

Even more distressing were the difficulties she found integrating into the l'Arche community. "At the beginning, I couldn't help feeling that I was just a fat bourgeois lady among the poor. Not only that, but I also felt utterly defeated by the place and, try as I did, I just couldn't feel a part of it. And I couldn't understand why."

Her breakthrough came one cool autumn night when she felt overcome by loneliness and despair. Seeking solace, she walked down the street to the l'Arche chapel, a simple room in a stone building lit only by a small candle burning on the altar. Pauline found herself alone in the chapel. She sat down on a bench and quite suddenly burst into tears. "Floods and floods of tears. I don't know what came over me, but I just felt so miserable. I felt such a fool about everything."

As she sat there, the door opened and one of the handicapped men came into the chapel. "He walked over and put his arm around my shoulder. Without saying a word, he took my hand and led me outside. Still clutching my hand, he walked me down the street to my home. He never said a single word, not one. But that's when I knew I was meant to be here. That's when I realized I was a very lucky woman to have found such a refuge in my old age, to have found love of such purity and simplicity."

This one small event proved an important breakthrough. "Suddenly I realized I had been trying too hard to understand the handicapped. I was trying in an intellectual way, feeling I had to rationalize their handicaps. What I was beginning to learn was simply to accept their inability to articulate, to open myself unreservedly to their need to communicate."

Almost at once, she began to win the love and affection of the whole community. Both those with handicaps and the assistants soon affectionately christened her "Mamie." Her warm and unfailing welcome and sympathetic ear became legends of the institution. So did the all-engulfing Vanier hug. "Her hugs are bestowed on anyone within reach of her welcoming arms and are easily the equal in efficacy of a pilgrimage to Lourdes," extolled John Fraser, after one of his many visits. Pauline Vanier had indeed found her role at l'Arche: as resident grandmother to the entire community.

For the handicapped, she in fact had become the grandmother they never knew, someone they could count on for uncritical acceptance, encouragement and a feeling of self-worth. For the assistants, she was their mother and best friend, someone to talk to or to laugh with, someone to offer them a word of comfort or a shoulder to cry on. "The fact that she was *always there* was so important to us all," said Barbara Swanekamp. "You just knew she was always there."

Hers was a magic touch that went a long way to help heal the wounds of loneliness or despair, homesickness or fear, especially among the assistants who were often far from home. She remembered who had a passion for chocolate mousse, donned her apron and whipped up her own secret recipe. She knew when a hefty dollop of pear jam would bring cheer. Or when a homemade muffin or a pot of Earl Grey tea (her own favourite) or even a cigarette (Gauloise *sans filtre*) would help ease the pangs of homesickness. Said one assistant who was feeling deeply depressed on her last visit: "Mamie didn't give me a long moralizing lecture. She just handed me a glass of cognac!"

Pauline Vanier's life at l'Arche was simple and carefully regulated. She was up at 6:00 a.m. every morning and spent at least an hour in morning prayers and as much time again in reading and in quiet reflection before breakfast, particularly during her first few years. She never missed the BBC world news at 9:00 a.m., then would settle into her voluminous correspondence. In later years, as her eyesight declined, she dictated her replies to a handful of regular visitors. Each letter was painstakingly thought-out beforehand, with every word and phrase chosen with care.

She loved to listen to music — Russian Orthodox church music was a favourite — or to one of the tapes of books or lectures supplied by friends. A voracious reader since childhood, she had read in recent years most of the 84 volumes of the "Fathers of the Church." But as her eyesight failed, she experienced an almost unbearable frustration that she could no longer read her favourite tomes. She listened, though, with rapt attention to readings on audio-cassettes; the last was a ten-part commentary on the Gospel of St. John by the French sister, Christella. Friends also read books to her, including such favourites as the autobiography of her long-time friend Elizabeth de Miribel and the writings of Thérèse of Lisieux.

A steady stream of visitors found their way to Les Marronniers: old friends and new, students and priests ("My, how I love those Jesuits!" she would exclaim, recalling the lively intellectual exchanges she would have with them). Former assistants came, as did politicians (former Canadian Prime Minister Pierre Trudeau came to see her with his three sons) and of course members of her far-flung family.

She greeted some visitors with the trepidation of a school child. "He has a Ph.D.in nuclear physics, you know," she would say, eyes rolling heavenwards. "What can I possibly say to him? I am not an intellectual." That did not stop her from challenging them with an endless succession of probing questions. "No one can accuse me of not having my own points of view," she once said. "I have an opinion on just about everything."

Assistants, too, were regular afternoon visitors and they marvelled at her insights into people and events. Hungarian assistant Klara Dorne, for example, recalls her first visit to tea. "She was incredibly interested in my country," she said. "In fact, she knew more about what was happening in Hungary than I did!"

Ellen Donnelly from Syracuse, New York, was equally impressed. She had been in the community just three days when she received a telephone call from Pauline Vanier inviting her to lunch. "I was amazed she found me so quickly," said Ellen. "I was really nervous, knowing who she was. But it was like meeting a really good friend. She made me feel completely at home, asked me a lot of questions and by the end of lunch, she knew my whole life history."

This was the first of what became weekly visits that nourished them both. "Whenever I arrived, she always said to me: 'I don't know why you bother to come to see an old lady like me. I don't really feel I am useful any longer or that I am doing any good.' I would try to tell her how important she was to so many of us in the community, specially the younger assistants, and she would always seem to be really surprised."

Ellen continued these weekly visits till the end of Pauline's life. One afternoon, she asked Mamie what it was like to be 92. "It's nothing like being 22," she laughed, and added, "It is like being at the edge of a precipice. You don't know what will happen tomorrow. All I have to do is to wait and pray!"

It was not only the assistants she helped, however. She also brought a motherly understanding to many of their parents, some of whom were perplexed about their child's decision to work at l'Arche. "She has had so much experience with her own children, especially since one of them became a Trappist monk," said Alain Saint-Macary, director of the community. "She was the best person to help these parents. She knew what they were going through because she had been through it all herself."

That same sensitivity helped her recognize that the English-speaking assistants often missed worshipping in their own language. So she frequently transformed her own small sitting room into a tiny chapel, placing on a table an open Bible, a silver cross and a tiny candle. And most Thursday nights for over four years she welcomed English-speaking assistants of all faiths to her informal prayer meetings. Up to two dozen young people knocked on her door at 9:30 p.m, sat on cushions on the floor and, for over an hour, listened to taped lectures, usually John Main on "centring prayer," prayed aloud or silently, and sang a favourite hymn together. It was one of Pauline Vanier's own personal contributions to l'Arche and she treasured those meetings. Said Sue Mosteller, who attended some of them: "For so many, this was a spirituality they could understand, one that was clear and simple and offered in their own language.

"But it was also a moment of being home, a respite from a culture that wasn't theirs. It was warm, it was safe. Mamie offered spiritual safety to so many people. In fact, she gave such re-assurance to people that they just poured their hearts out to her.

"For others of us, it was like coming back to the source. You felt refreshed for having been there. And in the quiet of that little room, people decided that, 'Yes, I should go to India,' or, 'I should take on this responsibility.' Indeed, many people's lives were transformed by those meetings."

One was that of Philip Kearney, an Irishman who lived for seven years as an assistant at l'Arche before he felt called to the priesthood. "When I first arrived at l'Arche, I attended all Mamie's Thursday evening prayer meetings," he said. "How she nourished us, not only with gingerbread and tea many afternoons, but through those evening prayer meetings. There is no doubt that my calling to become a priest matured through those meetings."

Two other events became important highlights to her week. Every Sunday, she wended her way through the back garden to the original l'Arche, now home to seven men with handicaps and as many assistants, to join them for Sunday lunch. She also turned up for every resident's birthday, arriving with a special word for each person. And on Saturday evenings she often dined at La Forestière, home for 10 of l'Arche's most severely handicapped members. Her favourite was Loic, a short child-like man of 35 who is so disabled he cannot feed or dress himself and seems unable to communicate. But Pauline Vanier was never inhibited by his isolation: she would sit down beside Loic, cuddle him in her arms and help feed him. "He knew that voice," said Alain Saint-Macary. "The minute she held him close to her, he would be perfectly calm. Over the years, she developed a very deep understanding of how to reach even the most severely handicapped."

As she struggled to develop this vital rapport with the handicapped around her, Pauline Vanier was also preoccupied with a constant search for her own identity. "In Canada, I was always Georges Vanier's wife. Here I am Jean Vanier's mother, and it is not easy being Jean Vanier's mother." But, little by little, she began to realize her own place in the l'Arche community. "Here at l'Arche, she discovered a real place for giving herself," recalled Cecilia MacPherson, an assistant who was offered "the enormous gift" of sharing Pauline's home for six years. "She knew her house was a place where people could open up their hearts. Before," she added, "her life seemed to be losing direction. L'Arche gave her a real purpose for living."

Right up until her death, Pauline Vanier still harboured doubts about her usefulness at l'Arche. But it is clear she found there a refuge for the emotional stresses of her later years and a satisfying outlet for her ever-youthful spirit.

"Yes, I am certainly kept young here," she said, well after her 90th birthday celebrations. "My stupid body won't keep up with my mind, but that's the same problem that most old people face...

"No, I've certainly got no cause for complaint. I've had a rich life full of gifts from God. I married Georges Vanier and that was the greatest gift of all, but coming to l'Arche is a very close second!"

Had she been able to speak at the moment of her death, she would undoubtedly have added a third, the most supreme of all. But the closer she came to that moment, the more difficult was the spiritual challenge she had first to overcome.

Pauline Vanier on her 90th birthday.

(L'Arche photo.)

Epilogue:
The End of the Journey

Once Pauline Vanier had found her niche at l'Arche, she seemed, to most people, to be a figure of imposing self-assurance, strength of conviction and serenity of faith. Those who were close to her, however, knew differently. There was a much more troubled side to her spiritual life, a deep anxiety and need of affirmation, that had plagued her since she was young, and came close to overwhelming her in the final years of her life.

There was certainly nothing forced about her vivacity and spontaneity, or about the depth of her love and concern for others. These were completely natural to her, required no effort of will on her part and, during most of her waking moments, took over her life completely.

In fact, she made others live, and live more fully, and they in return made her fully alive. She called forth the best in them, as they did in her.

But her long life, as one journalist noted, was "an unending spiritual quest," a continuing pilgrimage.

She needed regular reassurances from others to help still the anxieties that increased through her life, and redoubled with the infirmities of age. One such anxiety was that she would too soon exhaust all the love she had to give, and that some barrier would prevent her from surrendering herself in complete trust to the one transfusion that could renew her, the boundless, limitless love of her Creator.

Pauline Vanier shared these thoughts and fears with a few she called "fellow pilgrims" on the same spiritual journey. One was Lon Whitman, a young American assistant who had spent most Tuesday afternoons with her since his arrival at l'Arche two years earlier. "In our afternoons together," he recalls, "she talked often about the need she felt to be 'stripped' — stripped of all pretensions, of all self-indulgence and dependence on creature comforts, of her subconscious yearnings for her former influence and prestige, of all defences against spiritual intrusions. She wanted to be stripped as well of what she called her 'foolish self-reliance,' her imagined ability to do God's will without having to humble herself by asking His help.

"She once said it is these obstacles that prevented her from throwing herself on the love of God. She was already learning at l'Arche the humility of accepting poverty in physical things; she had to come as well to recognize the need for a similar poverty in spiritual matters.

"'I think our Lord is trying to teach me how to tear down these barriers,' she said on another occasion, 'to put my trust in Him rather than in my own abilities. But I am a slow learner. He has been obliged to take from me much of my physical strength and intellectual self-satisfaction to remind me just how dependent I really am on Him.

"'I know in my heart that I am a weak, small and broken person, but in my pride I still cannot strip away my own obstinacy, or abandon my defences against

His love. I simply cannot admit my spiritual emptiness, and surrender my heart, even less my soul, and much less my mind, to the one source that can restore me.'"

"How earnestly I prayed with her," Lon added, "that the Lord would finish the stripping away of those barriers that still held her prisoner."

She talked of these things often with close friends right up to a few days before her death. Her anxieties, one of these friends said, were not unlike those of Saint Thérèse of Lisieux, from whose writings both she and her husband had taken such comfort and inspiration. But while her husband had accepted unreservedly the omnipotence of divine love, Pauline's intellectual side always opposed the idea of the self-abandonment, the complete trust such acceptance involved.

Other spiritual advisors encouraged her to seek this self-abandonment. Father Michael Czerny, a Jesuit priest who visited her often at l'Arche, wrote a special prayer for her on her ninetieth birthday; she kept a copy of it close at hand, and repeated it daily, noting especially the parts which read, "We want to be entirely yours...to consecrate ourselves to your heart...May your love become the heart of our own lives..."

The inroads of age seemed almost divinely designed to encourage her in this direction, sapping her of her own physical capacities and independence. Each day, in her final years, she was becoming more frail and easily tired.

Reluctant to trust God's love wholly and exclusively, she became increasingly in need of reassurances of affection from those close to her, particularly Jean. She fought hard to avoid being overly dependent on him, especially as his duties with the ever-expanding l'Arche movement kept him abroad for long periods. One breakthrough in her spiritual journey was her success in transforming these possessive impulses into an active prayer life in support of Jean's missions overseas.

She also turned to her oldest son Benedict, still living as a Trappist monk, whose long and thoughtful letters, she once said, "always brought me back to the centre."

But still, many felt she needed to make one last, giant step in her spiritual journey before she would be ready to reach its end. None guessed, even a week before her death, how close she was to making that step, and the quite astonishing way it would come about.

Françoise Cambier, a French assistant at l'Arche, spent much time with Pauline in her last years, and was responsible for her day-to-day care. She provided great reassurance in moments of anxiety and, during Pauline's last days, she was never far from her side.

"In her last months, Mamie had become heavily dependent on assurances from Jean and others at l'Arche of their love for her," she recalled. "She was sick with misgiving as the week of the community's annual pilgrimage to Lourdes approached, because she would be left almost alone at l'Arche. And how she dreaded being alone. She had become so fragile, not only physically but emotionally, that her anxiety about being 'abandoned' for even a short period seemed almost to paralyse her."

Her daughter Thérèse came from London to be with her for part of that time. "During the week, there were highs and lows," Françoise remembers. "At first her fatigue seemed overwhelming, but she refused to rest in bed, insisting on being dressed and helped to walk about. Her son Bernard came with his daughters Valérie and Laurence for lunch on Sunday for a joint birthday celebration, and Mamie seemed cheerful and at ease.

"But on Monday, Tuesday and Wednesday she seemed very tired. Yet she put on such a brave face, that no one else, not even Thérèse, suspected how depressed she was. On Thursday morning, when Thérèse prepared to leave for a few days, her mother seemed buoyant and smiling, and urged her to go, assuring her that all was well."

Later, after Thérèse had left, Françoise checked up on her patient and was stunned by what she found. "Mamie was lying in bed curled up with her knees to her chin like a tiny child, shaking and sobbing. She could barely even speak."

Françoise sent at once for a doctor who discovered Pauline was not only in great mental anguish, but crushed with physical agony as well. The pain seemed centred in her digestive tract.

She clearly needed medical help, so, at about 1:00 p.m., an ambulance arrived to take her to the clinic.

From the first X-ray, it was clear that an immediate operation would be required: the doctor saw no other possible choice. But first it was necessary to undertake a series of tests.

The tests took more than six hours. She was first undressed and placed on a *brancard*, a hard, leather-covered steel stretcher mounted on wheels. Then she was wheeled to one room for extensive X-rays, to another for drawing blood samples, to another for various internal examinations, and to yet others for the interminable interrogation about her medical history.

Between the cold and seemingly callous adminis-tration of these tests, she was partially covered with a light sheet and moved back out to the drafty hallway. "I noticed she was shivering with cold, and I begged for a blanket to cover her," said Françoise. "Then, after long pleading, I was able to have her transferred to a bed in a vacant room so she could have some rest until her next tests. The 'rest' lasted five minutes before she was moved again.

"The afternoon was long and agonizing: the dis-comfort of the *brancard*, the long periods of waiting in the corridors, the painful tests added to all the mental anguish involved were almost impossible to stand. How desperately I wanted all these sufferings to stop.

"But then, as I looked closely at Mamie, I found her completely peaceful, serene, even smiling! She would not hear of me making the least protest, and throughout her ordeal never once murmured even the smallest complaint."

Could it be that she had attained what she had longed for, that she had at last been *stripped* of all her dignities and defences, and surrendered herself to God in complete trust, serene in the knowledge that God would accept her just as she was?

She seemed bathed in peacefulness, and so she remained, Françoise remembers, until the last tests were over. She even relaxed the aloofness of the doctors with questions about their families and gentle humour. With one earnest young intern who was examining her, she added a touch of mischievous coquetry: "Look at these beautiful legs, Doctor! Tell me they're not the legs of a fifteen-year-old!"

In the end the tests seemed superfluous, for the X-rays had already told the doctors all they needed to know — Pauline Vanier was stricken with widespread intestinal cancer. If she were to survive the night she would need an operation immediately. The likelihood of her living through a major operation at her age was remote, but it was even more unlikely she could last even a few more hours without one. It was decided to proceed at once.

Her children were contacted and they reached her by telephone during the afternoon. A special concession from the hospital allowed Jean and close friends from l'Arche to visit her that evening after the operation. She remained, of course, unconscious throughout the visit and the whole night.

In the morning, she regained consciousness momentarily. She opened her eyes, and recognized Jean at her side. She could not speak because her mouth was filled with tubes. But she did not need words, because her eyes spoke volumes. They had suddenly become again the eyes of a young girl, radiant, shining, and at peace. They spoke for all by her bedside of deep and consoling reassurance. But above all, they spoke of her complete trust, and of God's eternal, unrestrained love, filling her entire being and radiating to all those present.

Her message transmitted, she relapsed into unconsciousness and died shortly thereafter. Pauline Vanier's long pilgrimage had at last reached its fulfilment.

MARQUIS

PRINTED BY THE WORKERS OF
IMPRIMERIE D'ÉDITION MARQUIS
IN DECEMBER 1994
MONTMAGNY (QUÉBEC)